Daily Inspirations From God's Word

A 365 Day Mini Devotional

Doreen Wennberg

Fruit of the Vine Publishing

Daily Inspirations From God's Word

A 365 Day Mini Devotional

Copyright © 2018 by Doreen Wennberg-1st ed.

www.doreenwennberg.com

ISBN:13: 978-0-9995905-0-8

LCCN: 2018912820

Fruit of the Vine Publishing

A special thank you to all those who have been faithful to pray this project to completion. Your prayers have meant so much and I thank God for each of you.

To my husband Scott, thank you for your love, prayers, and support in allowing me the endless hours needed for this project. Thank you for pushing me forward, I love you!

To my daughter Kacy, you have been one of my greatest cheerleaders! Thank you. Your sweet encouragement is precious to me. Love you honey!

To my son David, thank you for rallying behind me, supporting me, and helping with technical issues. Love you buddy!

To my daughter-in-law Brittany, you married a great guy, and he's lucky to have you! Thank you for giving us two beautiful grandbaby girls, Leila and Zoe. Love each of you!

All praise to the Lord as He has faithfully guided me through every step big and small. Thank you for growing me through this project. Your love and grace are amazing!

Daily
Inspirations
From
God's Word

A 365 Day Mini Devotional

Daily Inspirations From God's Word

January 1

You make known to me the path of life; you will fill me with joy in your presence, with eternal pleasures at your right hand.

~ Psalm 16:11 NIV

In this coming new year, as you seek God and spend time in his presence, ask him for direction for your life. He is faithful; he will fill you with joy as he shows you the path to take.

January 2

"For I know the plans I have for you," declares the LORD, "plans to prosper you and not to harm you, plans to give you hope and a future."

~ Jeremiah 29:11

God has a good plan for your life. Although the past year may have been filled with trials, look ahead to the future. We always have hope when we look to God to lead us.

January 3

Consider it pure joy, my brothers and sisters, whenever you face trials of many kinds, because you know that the testing of your faith produces perseverance. ~ James 1;2-3 NIV

Don't be *surprised* when trials cross your path this year. They are part of God's plan to strengthen your faith in Him. The key to facing trials is to stay positive in the midst of them. The joy comes when we see how we've grown through our trials.

Daily Inspirations From God's Word

January 4

Like a city whose walls are broken through is a person who lacks self-control.

~ Proverbs 25:28 NIV

In Bible times cities were protected from enemies by walls. If the walls were broken, the enemy could gain entrance. Weak areas in our lives leave us vulnerable too. If you struggle with a lack of self-control, pray that God will give you restraint and the strength to overcome.

January 5

So then, let us not be like others, who are asleep, but let us be alert and self-controlled.

~1 Thessalonians 5:6 NIV

Many people in the world are indifferent to spiritual things. Believers should care about the things of God. We watch, pray and stay on guard. When we apply God's Word, it helps us control wrong behavior.

January 6

But since we belong to the day, let us be self-controlled, putting on faith and love as a breast-plate, and the hope of salvation as a helmet.

~1 Thessalonians 5:8

Walking in faith, hope, and love and putting on God's armor are important weapons against spiritual enemies. Protect your heart by applying the breastplate and loving others. Your spiritual helmet is the hope of salvation, which defends your mind. A warrior is prepared, on guard, and self-controlled. Are you?

Daily Inspirations From God's Word

January 7

For the grace of God has appeared that offers salvation to all people. It teaches us to say "No" to ungodliness, and to live self-controlled, upright and godly lives in this present age.

~Titus 2:11-12 NIV

Living as a Christian is counter-cultural. We live different than the world does and care more about what God thinks than what others think. We learn this by denying ourselves the instant gratification we think we must have.

January 8

Therefore, prepare your minds for action; be self-controlled; set your hope fully on the grace to be given you when Jesus Christ is revealed.

~1 Peter 1:13 NIV

Choose to live this year mentally prepared for Christ's return. Live with restraint from worldliness and keep your focus on his coming.

January 9

The end of all things is near. Therefore be clear minded and self-controlled so that you can pray.
~ 1 Peter 4:7 NIV

We live in the last days. Now more than ever, our spirits need to be in tune with the Father's Spirit through prayer. Live so that you are alert and not distracted by the world's temptations.

January 10

Be self-controlled and alert. Your enemy the devil prowls around like a roaring lion looking for someone to devour. ~ 1 Peter 5:8 NIV

Daily Inspirations From God's Word

Predators choose vulnerable prey. Likewise, when we're tired, sick or spiritually weak, we leave ourselves open to attack. Satan sees our weakness and pursues. Keep watch and be on guard, so that you are not wiped out.

January 11

Therefore, since we are surrounded by such a great cloud of witnesses, let us throw off everything that hinders and the sin that so easily entangles, and let us run with perseverance the race marked out for us. ~ Hebrews 12:1 NIV

What have you set out to do this year that the enemy has opposed? Don't give up. Be encouraged by those who've gone before you, who also have struggled with Satan trying to hinder their goals. What attitudes, practices or activities may you need to drop that are disabling you from your goals? Running requires endurance to go the distance. Persist in the face of difficulty and you too will win.

January 12

You know that the testing of your faith develops perseverance. ~James 1:3 NIV

God allows trials in our lives to test us. Faith and perseverance do not grow automatically. We build them up by walking steadily and by continuing in spite of opposition.

January 13

Perseverance must finish its work so that you may be mature and complete, not lacking anything. ~ James 1:4 NIV

Daily Inspirations From God's Word

God continues to grow our character to bring us to spiritual maturity in Christ. Pressure may cause us to react in anger, with impatience, or doubt. But the quality of remaining steadfast under pressure conveys mature faith.

January 14

Blessed is the man who perseveres under trial, because when he has stood the test, he will receive the crown of life that God has promised to those who love him. ~ James 1:12 NIV

Doing something over and over in the face of great difficulty is hard. Working with or loving unreasonable people isn't easy, but our character shines forth by what we say and do. When we are under pressure, God sees and rewards us for persisting through the hardship.

Daily Inspirations From God's Word

January 15

As you know, we consider blessed those who have persevered. You have heard of Job's perseverance and have seen what the Lord finally brought about. ~James 5:11 NIV

Job's example of strength under fire is without comparison. He lost everything; his children, his home, his wealth, and his health. But Job didn't lose his faith or his love for God. Job didn't love God only when life was good. Job persevered because no matter what God allowed in his life, he knew God loved him and he knew God is good. If we are assured of God's love, we can stand strong like Job did.

January 16

May the Lord direct your hearts into God's love and Christ's perseverance.

~ 2Thessalonians 3:5 NIV

Daily Inspirations From God's Word

The Lord Jesus left us many examples to follow. One of them is perseverance. Jesus patiently endured the crowds demands, endless ministry, schooling his disciples, and relentless badgering from the religious leaders. God wants us to have a full understanding of his love for us. Like Jesus, we *can* persevere through difficult things when we lean on the one who loves us.

January 17

But the seed on good soil stands for those with a noble and good heart, who hear the word, retain it, and by persevering produce a crop.

~Luke 8:15 NIV

Every farmer knows that to produce a crop, he must start with good soil. A lot of work goes into getting a crop. A farmer must continue day after day growing, working his crop in spite of drought, pests, or weeds. As the Word of God – the seed – takes root in your heart, continue working to retain it. Study and apply the Word, so it will produce a fruitful harvest in your life.

January 18

"Then you call on the name of your god, and I will call on the name of the LORD. The god who answers by fire – he is God."

~1 Kings 18:24 NIV

Elijah challenged the people to see if their god, Baal or the LORD God, would set fire to the bulls the heathen had sacrificed on the altar. Elijah trusted in the one true God. He knew God would answer. Many people put their trust in false gods that can do nothing. But when we put our trust in the LORD God, we find He is faithful.

Daily Inspirations From God's Word

January 19

Before they call I will answer; while they are still speaking I will hear. ~ Isaiah 65:24 NIV

God knows our hearts and our thoughts before we even speak them. He hears our prayers. God is always ready to answer. Even before we know we have a need, He anticipates our call.

January 20

Call to me and I will answer you and tell you great and unsearchable things you do not know.
~ Jeremiah 33:3 NIV

God is always encouraging us to communicate with him. The LORD God personally, speaks to us through his Word and prayer. He has an answer for every need and gives us understanding for our questions. You can trust God to do what he says he will do.

Daily Inspirations From God's Word

January 21

He determines the number of stars and calls them each by name. ~ Psalm 147:4 NIV

There is no one who compares with God, the Creator of the Universe. Everything came into being at His command. When you look at the stars, what do you see? Do you search the heavens and marvel at the One who created all these, who gave each one its name? Praise God for His awesome creation!

January 22

On hearing this, Jesus said to them, "It is not the healthy who need a doctor, but the sick. I have not come to call the righteous, but sinners."

~ Mark 2:17 NIV

When Jesus came to earth, he was here for one reason: to redeem mankind from sin.

Daily Inspirations From God's Word

Jesus came for all people, rich and poor, good and bad. Do you ever think of the people some in society consider bad? Would you sit and eat with a drunk or homeless person? How about a drug addict or a prostitute? Jesus did, because loving sinful people is the pathway that leads them to realize their need of Him.

January 23

For there is no difference between Jew and Gentile – the same Lord is Lord of all and richly blesses all who call on him.

~ Romans 10:12 NIV

It doesn't matter who you are when you come to God. His love is the same for all who call upon his name. God is no respecter of persons.

Daily Inspirations From God's Word

January 24

But you are a chosen people, a royal priesthood,
a holy nation, God's special possession, that you
may declare the praises of him who called you
out of darkness into his wonderful light.

~ 1 Peter 2:9 NIV

God uses descriptive words about those who
belong to him. People who once lived a life
contrary to His ways, know the joy of being
born again and changed. The proof is, their
lives praise Him.

January 25

But these are written that you may believe that
Jesus is the Messiah, the Son of God, and that by
believing you may have life in his name.

~ John 20:31 NIV

Not all the works and miracles of Jesus were

recorded. Those that were written help us understand and believe who Jesus is. Our eternal life is dependent on our belief in God's Son. It is not by works that we receive eternal life, but by faith in the name of Jesus Christ.

January 26

Whoever believes in the Son has eternal life.

~ John 3:36a NIV

Many people claim to believe in God. The belief in God's Son, Jesus, is what sets Christianity apart from other religions. Do you know the Son? Believe in Jesus Christ, and he will give you eternal life with him.

Daily Inspirations From God's Word

January 27

That if you confess with your mouth, "Jesus is Lord," and believe in your heart that God raised him from the dead, you will be saved.

~ Romans 10:9 NIV

God's grace draws us to an understanding of the scriptures. We voice our belief in the One who came to give life, and by the gift of faith we come to believe in Jesus.

January 28

Then the man said, "Lord, I believe," and he worshiped him. ~ John 9:38 NIV

Something happens *in* us when we believe. We have an inner awareness that Jesus is Who he said he is. By faith we understand that Jesus is now a part of us, and our hearts are changed.

Daily Inspirations From God's Word

January 29

Jesus said to her, "I am the resurrection and the life. The one who believes in me will live, even though they die, and whoever lives by believing in me will never die. Do you believe this?"

~ John 11:25-26 NIV

When Jesus rose from the dead he defeated death. Every person will eventually die in this life. Where you live in eternity is determined by what you believe while here. Jesus came to give life to all who believe in him, so that they will live forever with him.

January 30

"Yes, Lord," she told him, "I believe that you are the Christ, the Son of God, who was to come into the world." ~ John 11:27 NIV

Mary confessed her belief that Jesus is the Christ, God's Son. When you come to believe in Jesus, you acknowledge who He is.

January 31

Then he said to Thomas, "Put your finger here; see my hands. Reach out your hand and put it into my side. Stop doubting and believe."

~ John 20:27 NIV

Some people need to see before they believe, but faith is believing in what you can't see. In John 20:29 Jesus said, "blessed are those who have not seen and yet believed." Our belief in Jesus shows trust, acceptance, and faith.

Daily Inspirations From God's Word

February 1

The fear of the Lord is the beginning of wisdom, and knowledge of the Holy One is understanding. ~ Proverbs 9:10 NIV

Some people in this world have no fear of God. They do as they please without thought of the consequences. But those who begin to read and study God's Word learn that He's a Holy God. They fear displeasing Him. Out of respect and reverence for the Lord they choose not to sin.

February 2

For it is written: "Be holy, because I am holy."
~ 1 Peter 1:16 NIV

God commands His children to live differently than people in the world do. Holiness means being set apart, so living holy is living separate from sin and evil. God calls us to be like Him, and because we are his children we should reflect His holiness.

February 3

"Do not come any closer," God said. "Take off your sandals, for the place where you are standing is holy ground." ~ Exodus 3:5 NIV

There are times when you and I encounter the powerful presence of the Lord. When that happens, we become aware that we are to behave differently. In Moses' day, people took their shoes off before entering a home out of respect and because of the dust and dirt their feet had picked up on the roads.

God's command to Moses was essentially saying, "don't bring dirt into my presence, but come into my presence with reverence."

Daily Inspirations From God's Word

February 4

But among you there must not be even a hint of sexual immorality, or of any kind of impurity, or of greed, because these are improper for God's holy people. ~ Ephesians 3:5 NIV

Images of sexual immorality and lust for more on TV, the internet and magazines saturate our world today. These images influence and desensitize us to wrong behavior. God calls His people to live differently than the world does. How closely does our life resemble that difference and what positive examples are we setting for new believers who are just learning what this means?

February 5

Make every effort to live in peace with all men and to be holy; without holiness no one will see the Lord. ~ Hebrews 12:14 NIV

Daily Inspirations From God's Word

A life characterized by strife and sinful deeds is opposite of what Jesus desires for His followers. He calls us to make a conscious effort to live in a way that pleases Him. What areas might we need to bring to the Lord so He can help us change?

February 6

Each of the four living creatures had six wings and was covered with eyes all around, even under its wings. Day and night they never stop saying: "Holy, holy, holy is the Lord God Almighty, who was, and is, and is to come."

~ Revelation 4:8 NIV

There are many attributes that describe God. In this verse we hear one, over and over again. "Holy, holy, holy is the Lord God Almighty, who was, and is, and is to come." The image of the creatures as they repeat this is a powerful vision of our God who is eternal, and mighty, moving us to worship Him in all His splendor and holiness.

February 7

Therefore, since we have these promises, dear friends, let us purify ourselves from everything that contaminates body and spirit, perfecting holiness out of reverence for God.

~2 Corinthians 7:1 NIV

Sin defiles people. God calls his people to be pure. What in your and my life may need to be examined and cleansed, so that we can walk in holiness out of love and respect for God?

Daily Inspirations From God's Word

February 8

For God so loved the world that he gave his one and only Son, that whoever believes in him shall not perish but have eternal life.

~ John 3:16 NIV

The greatest example of love is God the Father who chose to give his Son to the world.

February 9

But God demonstrates his own love for us in this: While we were still sinners, Christ died for us.

~ Romans 5:8 NIV

There is no greater love than the love of someone who lays down his life for us.

Daily Inspirations From God's Word

February 10

Dear friends, let us love one another, for love comes from God. Everyone who loves has been born of God and knows God. ~ 1 John 4:7 NIV

God calls us to love others. Because God put his love in us, we can love even the most difficult people. Are people in your life hard to love? Ask God to pour more love in you. He will!

February 11

Above all, love each other deeply, because love covers over a multitude of sins. ~ 1 Peter 4:8 NIV

When someone sins against us, love may not be our first thought toward them. But God calls us to love and cover – not expose – an offense. In all these things we need God's help. Ask him to help you love others deeply.

Daily Inspirations From God's Word

February 12

"For this reason, a man will leave his father and mother and be united to his wife, and the two will become one flesh." ~ Ephesians 5:31 NIV

According to this Scripture, when a man and woman marry, something unique happens. They separate from their parents, they unite to each other and they become one flesh. All three must happen for harmony in marriage.

February 13

He answered, "'Love the Lord your God with all your heart and with all your soul and with all your strength and with all your mind'; and, 'Love your neighbor as yourself.'" ~Luke10:27 NIV

Jesus says we are to love God with all that we have and to love others – our neighbors – as we love ourselves. When we do, we put God first, other people second and ourselves last. Where might our priorities need to change?

February 14

Love is patient and kind. Love is not jealous or boastful or proud or rude. It does not demand its own way. It is not irritable, and it keeps no record of being wronged. ~ 1 Corinthians 13:4-5 NLT

Three out of the nine fruits of the Spirit are mentioned in this verse – love, patience, and kindness. Each one is necessary to counteract the wrong behaviors of jealousy, boasting, and pride. When people persist in being irritable, demanding their way, and keeping track of others' faults, they're lacking love. The fruits of God's Spirit are evident in the believer when they are walking in love.

Daily Inspirations From God's Word

February 15

Do not deprive each other except perhaps by mutual consent and for a time, so that you may devote yourselves to prayer. Then come together again so that Satan will not tempt you because of your lack of self-control. ~ *1 Corinthians 7:5 NIV*

Sex is God's gift to married people. Paul even calls it a right for both husband and wife. But there are times when a couple can mutually decide to refrain for a time as they devote themselves to prayer. Perhaps for a troubled teen crisis, or a family member with cancer, or some other dire situation in which extended prayer is needed.

February 16

Jacob was in love with Rachel and said to her father, "I'll work for you seven years in return for your younger daughter Rachel." So Jacob served seven years to get Rachel, but they seemed like only a few days to him because of his love for her. ~ Genesis 29:18,20 NIV

Jacob was willing to wait many years for Rachel. In fact, he waited until he married Rachel to make love to her. (Gen 29:21, 27) Many people don't understand waiting to have sex. God gives specific guidelines when it comes to sex before marriage, and they are for our benefit.

February 17

It is God's will that you should be sanctified: that you should avoid sexual immorality; that each of you should learn to control your own body in a way that is holy and honorable, not in passionate lust like the pagans, who do not know God.

~ 1 Thessalonians 4:3-5 NIV

Waiting to be intimate till after marriage means being able to exercise control. Many people – even believers – do not avoid sexual immorality. Since it is God's will for us to be set apart – sanctified – believers are called to exhibit the fruit of self-control (Galatians 5:22-23). We are to be holy as He is holy.

February 18

Dear friends, I urge you, as foreigners and exiles, to abstain from sinful desires, which wage war against your soul. ~ 1 Peter 2:11 NIV

Christians are called by God to live differently than an unbelieving society. Refusing sinful behavior protects us from the corruption it causes.

Daily Inspirations From God's Word

February 19

The one who has knowledge uses words with restraint. ~ Proverbs 27:17a NIV

People who blurt out harsh words cause division and strife. Withholding angry words to diffuse circumstances is a wise choice.

February 20

Where there is no revelation, people cast off restraint; but blessed is the one who heeds wisdom's instruction. ~ Proverbs 29:18 NIV

People without vision from God often come to ruin, but those who follow God's instruction are blessed.

Daily Inspirations From God's Word

February 21

For the grace of God has appeared that offers salvation to all people. It teaches us to say "No" to ungodliness and worldly passions, and to live self-controlled, upright and godly lives in this present age. ~ Titus 2:11-12 NIV

The present age of ungodliness lives without restraint; therefore, they do as they please. Godly parents use boundaries and model for their children how to live differently than those who don't know God.

February 22

When I heard these things, I sat down and wept. For some days I mourned and fasted and prayed before the God of heaven. ~ Nehemiah 1:4 NIV

Fasting is not only an ancient practice. The scriptures teach us to fast and pray. Nehemiah mourned the news of Jerusalem's exiles and its broken, burned down walls. While there are many different reasons to fast and pray, very often it is for a breakthrough in hearing from God. When we deprive the body of food, it draws us closer so that our sole dependence is on God. We humble ourselves through fasting and our Spirit within is strengthened.

February 23

There, by the Ahava Canal, I proclaimed a fast, so that we might humble ourselves before our God and ask him for a safe journey for us and our children, with all our possessions.

~ Ezra 8:21NIV

Often scriptures show us that groups fasted together. Here, Ezra calls for a fast before a journey, and they humbled themselves before God. In a culture saturated with entitlement,

Daily Inspirations From God's Word

how might proclaiming a fast to refrain from food strengthen our dependence on and relationship with God?

February 24

The Pharisee stood by himself and prayed: 'God, I thank you that I am not like other people—robbers, evildoers, adulterers—or even like this tax collector. I fast twice a week and give a tenth of all I get.' ~ Luke 18:11-12 NIV

We fast in humility towards God, not out of self-righteousness.

February 25

"How can the guests of the bridegroom mourn while he is with them? The time will come when

the bridegroom will be taken from them; then they will fast." ~ Matthew 9:15 NIV

Jesus' disciples did not fast while he was with them. This scripture shows his reply when the Pharisees challenged him. If anyone today questions the spiritual discipline of fasting, Jesus himself shows the necessity for it.

February 26

While they were worshiping the Lord and fasting, the Holy Spirit said, "Set apart for me Barnabas and Saul for the work to which I have called them." ~ Acts 13:2 NIV

God gives instructions during fasting and prayer. Worshiping, fasting, and praying bring us into a closer union with the Lord where we receive insight and direction.

Daily Inspirations From God's Word

February 27

Paul and Barnabas appointed elders for them in each church and, with prayer and fasting, committed them to the Lord, in whom they had put their trust. ~ Acts 14:23 NIV

There are times to celebrate with feasting and times to humble ourselves with fasting. Paul and Barnabas perceived that the two acts of prayer and fasting preceded appointments of sincere and serious work for the Lord.

February 28

So we fasted and petitioned our God about this, and he answered our prayer. ~ Ezra 8:23 NIV

Fasting is not some magical formula. It is an emptying of *self* and dependence upon God to hear or discern from Him.

Daily Inspirations From God's Word

March 1

This is the confidence we have in approaching God: that if we ask anything according to his will, he hears us. ~ 1 John 5:14 NIV

How should we approach God? First, with a clear conscience by confessing sin. Our confidence comes from knowing we are in right standing with God. Second, asking for *anything* does not mean we will get whatever we ask just because we want it. We are to submit to God's will, not our own. He hears the prayer of faith, so pray with confidence, *in* faith.

March 2

Look to the Lord and his strength; seek his face always. ~ 1 Chronicles 16:11 NIV

Who do you look to for the direction in your life, or when crisis strikes? There are many popular places to turn to for help these days. Google gives us a lot of information. Social media is full of advice from well-meaning friends. But there is no person on earth who knows you intimately like the Lord knows you. There is no substitute for the strength that he alone can give.

March 3

Take the helmet of salvation and the sword of the Spirit, which is the word of God. And pray in the Spirit on all occasions with all kinds of prayers and requests. With this in mind, be alert and always keep on praying for all the Lord's people.
~Ephesians 6:17-18 NIV

A soldier's helmet protects his head. In the spiritual realm, the mind within our head—that's where Satan does battle. The sword of the Spirit is both defensive and offensive. Defensively it blocks the enemy's weapon; offensively it is what the soldier attacks with. The sword *is* the Word of God. Speaking scripture out loud is using the sword. It is what Jesus used during temptation to defeat the enemy in the desert. Praying in the Spirit is praying *in* the power of and *by* the leading of the Spirit. A spiritual soldier is always to be on alert and lift in prayer the people of God.

March 4

Is anyone among you in trouble? Let them pray.
~ *James 5:13a NIV*

When you see trouble ahead, is your first thought to pray? Many scriptures tell us to pray. God hears when we call to Him. Activate your faith and know that He is able to help you through your trouble.

March 5

And when you pray, do not keep on babbling like pagans, for they think they will be heard because of their many words.

~ Matthew 6:7 NIV

It is not necessary to go on and on giving every detail when we pray. Concise, specific sentences will do – God knows what we need before we ask Him. But He wants us to ask.

March 6

I call on you, my God, for you will answer me; turn your ear to me and hear my prayer.

~ Psalm 17:6 NIV

There may be times when we feel God has not heard our prayer. He seems silent. But like the Psalmist, keep pressing in. Don't take the silence for inactivity; God is always working –

Daily Inspirations From God's Word

He just may not have revealed His answer to you yet.

March 7
The prayer of a righteous person is powerful and effective. ~ James 5:16b NIV

Have you ever thought that *your* prayer could be powerful and effective in someone's life? When God calls His servants to pray, it is *in* His name and *by* His Word, His righteousness, and His power that we pray. That's what makes it effective. How effectively are you praying?

March 8
All wrongdoing is sin, and there is sin that does not lead to death. ~ 1 John 5:17 NIV

Daily Inspirations From God's Word

All people—even those who believe in Christ—can and will still sin. The sin *leading to death* is a hard-hearted, unrepentant heart. Sins that *do not lead to death as* talked about here are the wrong things most of us do, but we repent from them. We don't remain in them.

March 9

For the sinful nature desires what is contrary to the Spirit, and the Spirit what is contrary to the sinful nature. ~ Galatians 5:17a NIV

There's a long list in Galatians 5:19-21 which characterizes those following after the flesh. A person who knows Christ can have the Spirit *in* him, but not be walking *by* it. If we are walking *by* the Spirit we will do *as* the Spirit leads. Who's leading you?

Daily Inspirations From God's Word

March 10

For all have sinned and fall short of the glory of God. ~ Romans 3:23 NIV

The verse doesn't say *some*, it says *all*, because every one of us misses the mark or sins with either wrong thoughts, attitudes, or actions. To fall short of God's glory is to fail to be approved by Him because of our sinfulness.

March 11

God made him who had no sin to be sin for us, so that in him we might become the righteousness of God. ~ 2Corinthians 5:21 NIV

In and of ourselves, because of our sinful state, people have no righteousness. But Jesus Christ, who was sinless, became sin for us. Jesus gives his righteousness to all who believe in Him, so that we are now approved by God.

March 12

Put to death, therefore, whatever belongs to your earthly nature: sexual immorality, impurity, lust, evil desires and greed, which is idolatry.

~ Colossians 3:5 NIV

Like the pulling up of weeds, we can kill off all sins in our lives. God will help us make a conscious decision to uproot anything in our sinful nature that would hinder our walk with Him.

March 13

For the wages of sin is death, but the gift of God is eternal life in Christ Jesus our Lord.

~ Romans 6:23 NIV

Daily Inspirations From God's Word

There is no payment a man could give for his sin, except his life, but our death will not earn us eternal life. Our holy God will not accept a sinful person. But He gave the precious gift of the sinless Lord Jesus, who paid the price for our sin by giving His own life for all who believe in Him.

March 14

Therefore, since we are surrounded by such a great cloud of witnesses, let us throw off everything that hinders and the sin that so easily entangles. ~ Hebrews 12:1 NIV

Many heroes of the faith have gone before us bearing witness to the Christian faith. Every believer is running his or her own race. If we are tied up by any sin, we can't move forward freely. This Scripture instructs us to get rid of anything that will hinder our progress.

March 15

But because of your stubbornness and your unrepentant heart, you are storing up wrath against yourself for the day of God's wrath, when his righteous judgment will be revealed.

~Romans 2:5 NIV

There are people in every age who stubbornly refuse to humble themselves and admit their sin. One day, God will judge mankind for refusing to turn away from sin *to* him. Make a choice now to repent from your sin and turn to God.

Daily Inspirations From God's Word

March 16

The Lord is not slow in keeping his promise, as some understand slowness. Instead he is patient with you, not wanting anyone to perish, but everyone to come to repentance.

~ 2 Peter 3:9 NIV

One thing we can be sure of; the Lord is never late. He will come – no doubt. Will you be ready?

March 17

Jesus answered them, "It is not the healthy who need a doctor, but the sick. I have not come to call the righteous, but sinners to repentance."

~ Luke 5:31-32 NIV

Jesus spent time with many different people, among them tax collectors and prostitutes. Why? Because he loves everyone. The people who need to know the truth most are those who don't know it – those who need healing in body and soul. If our "church crowd" is the only crowd we hang out with, we must be willing to step outside it to help others know their need of Jesus and lead them to repentance.

March 18

Repent, then, and turn to God, so that your sins may be wiped out, that times of refreshing may come from the Lord. ~ Acts 3:19 NIV

The truth that our sins will be wiped out is wonderful. But notice the condition; we must first repent of our sin and turn to God. When we do that, God promises that we will indeed experience refreshing from the Lord.

Daily Inspirations From God's Word

March 19

For John came to you to show you the way of righteousness, and you did not believe him, but the tax collectors and the prostitutes did. And even after you saw this, you did not repent and believe him. ~ Matthew 21:32 NIV

Speaking to the Pharisees, Jesus pointed out that our actions speak louder than our words. Many people claim to know God, but their life doesn't show it.

March 20

Godly sorrow brings repentance that leads to salvation and leaves no regret, but worldly sorrow brings death. ~ 2 Corinthians 7:10 NIV

Regret causes a person to question why they did what they did. Remorse causes a person to feel upset at their sin. Neither brings about a change. Judas had both but he never repented,

Daily Inspirations From God's Word

and it led to spiritual death; separation from God. True repentance causes us to have a change of will/heart. This is godly sorrow, which leads to repentance, which leads to salvation.

March 21

For I take no pleasure in the death of anyone, declares the Sovereign Lord. Repent and live!
~Ezekiel 18:32 NIV

God says He will judge each of us according to our ways (Ezekiel 18:30). He takes no delight in a person's death. His heart is that none would perish. But because of man's sin, we will all die not only physically but spiritually *unless* we turn to God and repent. When we do, we'll live eternally with Him!

Daily Inspirations From God's Word

March 22

If we confess our sins, he is faithful and just and will forgive us our sins and purify us from all unrighteousness. ~ 1 John 1:9 NIV

Confession is our part – acknowledging to God what we've done wrong. Once we've done that sincerely, God faithfully forgives us and we are cleansed.

March 23

"I, even I, am he who blots out your transgressions, for my own sake, and remembers your sins no more. ~ Isaiah 43:25 NIV

People tend to repeatedly ask forgiveness for the same sins, but the scripture reminds us that God forgets them. Let us rejoice in that truth.

Daily Inspirations From God's Word

March 24

"Come now, let us settle the matter," says the LORD. "Though your sins are like scarlet, they shall be as white as snow; though they are red as crimson, they shall be like wool.

~ Isaiah 1:18 NIV

White represents purity. When the Lord forgives our sins, he changes us. He makes us pure.

March 25

In him we have redemption through his blood, the forgiveness of sins, in accordance with the riches of God's grace. ~ Ephesians 1:7 NIV

No one has righteousness in and of themselves. It is only through the shed blood of Jesus Christ that we are forgiven.

Daily Inspirations From God's Word

March 26
The Lord our God is merciful and forgiving, even though we have rebelled against him.

~ Daniel 9:9 NIV

In Daniel's prayer (ch.9), he confessed not only the many sins of the people but that God is merciful and forgiving. God punishes and he is just. But in his great mercy he is willing to withhold judgment and cancel our debt (sin) because he is forgiving.

March 27
For he has rescued us from the dominion of darkness and brought us into the kingdom of the Son he loves, in whom we have redemption, the forgiveness of sins. ~ Colossians 1:13-14 NIV

We could do nothing to free ourselves from the kingdom of darkness. But Jesus Christ,

Daily Inspirations From God's Word

God's Son redeemed and rescued every believer, forgiving our sin and paying for it himself.

March 28

As far as the east is from the west, so far has he removed our transgressions from us.

~ Psalm 103:12 NIV

We cannot conceive how far the East is from the West. But that is how far our sins are removed from us—so far, they can no longer affect us anymore.

March 29

Then he took a cup, and when he had given thanks, he gave it to them, saying, "Drink from it, all of you. This is my blood of the covenant, which is poured out for many for the forgiveness of sins." ~ Matthew 26:27-28 NIV

Before Jesus was arrested and during his last supper with his disciples, he explained what we as believers now commemorate with communion – the remembrance of his blood poured out for the forgiveness of *our* sins. This solemn but meaningful time is for our reflection on what Christ actually did on our behalf.

March 30

He did not enter by means of the blood of goats and calves; but he entered the Most Holy Place once for all by his own blood, thus obtaining eternal redemption. ~ Hebrews 9:12 NIV

In the Old Testament God had established the means by which sins were forgiven. This foreshadowed what Christ, the High Priest, and the perfect Lamb would come to do.

March 31

How much more, then, will the blood of Christ, who through the eternal Spirit offered himself unblemished to God, cleanse our consciences from acts that lead to death, so that we may serve the living God! ~ Hebrews 9:14 NIV

If the blood of goats and calves sanctified people in an outward temporal sense, then the blood of Christ, the spotless Lamb of God— fully cleanses and frees the sinner for all eternity.

Daily Inspirations From God's Word

April 1

And they sang a new song, saying: "You are worthy to take the scroll and to open its seals, because you were slain, and with your blood you purchased for God persons from every tribe and language and people and nation.

~ Revelation 5:9 NIV

God's requirement for the payment of sin is death. Jesus Christ, as the spotless Lamb, met that requirement for all people when he gave his life as a ransom for mankind. Truly He is worthy!

April 2

Since we have now been justified by his blood, how much more shall we be saved from God's wrath through him! ~ Romans 5:9 NIV

It's because of Christ's shed blood that God declares the believer righteous in his sight.

Daily Inspirations From God's Word

That's why we are spared God's wrath. Hallelujah!

April 3

But now in Christ Jesus you who once were far away have been brought near by the blood of Christ. ~ Ephesians 2:13 NIV

The wall of sin separated us from God. But Jesus' sacrificial blood changed that, giving all believers access to God.

April 4

For you know that it was not with perishable things such as silver or gold that you were redeemed from the empty way of life handed down to you from your ancestors, but with the precious blood of Christ, a lamb without blemish or defect. ~1 Peter 1:18-19 NIV

What were we redeemed from? Peter is reminding us *what* our forefathers came from – once enslaved in Egypt and freed—then bound to the law which could not save them. Every precious stone is corruptible. But the precious blood of Jesus that bought us is incorruptible.

April 5

Because you will not abandon me to the realm of the dead, nor will you let your faithful one see decay. ~ Psalm16:10 NIV

This promise was prophesied hundreds of years before God faithfully delivered Jesus from the grave. Unlike our body, Christ's would not see decay because it was raised to life.

Daily Inspirations From God's Word

April 6

Jesus said to her, "I am the resurrection and the life. The one who believes in me will live, even though they die; and whoever lives by believing in me will never die. Do you believe this?"

~ John 11:25-26 NIV

In speaking to Mary before raising her brother Lazarus, Jesus explained that he would not only raise her brother to life, but all who believe in him. Do you believe that?

April 7

There was a violent earthquake, for an angel of the Lord came down from heaven and, going to the tomb, rolled back the stone and sat on it. His appearance was like lightning, and his clothes were white as snow. The guards were so afraid of him that they shook and became like dead men.

~ Matthew 28:2-4 NIV

Jesus is God. He didn't need the stone rolled away. A later scripture tells us he walked right through doors. No, this miracle was done so all would know – starting with the guards— that Jesus rose from the grave.

April 8

The angel said to the women, "Do not be afraid, for I know that you are looking for Jesus, who was crucified. He is not here; he has risen, just as he said. Come and see the place where he lay. Then go quickly and tell his disciples: 'He has risen from the dead and is going ahead of you into Galilee. ~ Matthew 28:5-6 NIV

The women at the tomb were the first among those who followed Jesus to hear that he had risen. They also had the privilege to be the first ones to share the good news. Like these women, we all are commanded to share what we've witnessed about Jesus. Who have you told?

April 9

He told them, "This is what is written: The Messiah will suffer and rise from the dead on the third day, and repentance for the forgiveness of sins will be preached in his name to all nations, beginning at Jerusalem. ~ Luke 24:46-47 NIV

Before his death, Jesus explained to the disciples what the scripture foretold. It happened just as he and the scriptures said it would.

April 10

And if the Spirit of him who raised Jesus from the dead is living in you, he who raised Christ from the dead will also give life to your mortal bodies because of his Spirit who lives in you.

~Romans 8:11 NIV

For all believers, the promise of receiving eternal life after death is as certain as Jesus' resurrection.

April 11

Christ Jesus who died—more than that, who was raised to life—is at the right hand of God and is also interceding for us. ~ Romans 8:34 NIV

There are two sides to the cross. The one side is remembering the horrific suffering Jesus Christ endured to pay for mankind's sin with his life. That was victory in itself. But the other side is the greater victory of Christ's resurrection. He conquered death and lives to intercede for us!

April 12

So also Abraham "believed God, and it was credited to him as righteousness."

~ Romans 3:6 NIV

Faith *is* believing. When God called him, Abraham had to trust and believe by faith – just as we do. Not one of us is righteous in and of ourselves. Nor was Abraham. Because Abraham believed, God acknowledged—or credited—to him as righteous. Before Christ was born, died, and resurrected, Abraham believed. What do you believe?

April 13

Clearly no one who relies on the law is justified before God, because "the righteous will live by faith." ~ Romans 3:11 NIV

Daily Inspirations From God's Word

Speaking to those who still followed the law, Paul points out that only those who truly walk

by faith are justified and righteous. By faith we are made right with God, not by works, attending church, memorizing scripture, having godly parents or anything else.

April 14

As it is written: "There is no one righteous, not even one. ~ Romans 3:10 NIV

Most Jews would argue this statement, for they kept the law. They thought themselves to be righteous. Many people today might also argue this statement. *I'm not bad.* Maybe not, but have you never sinned? And that's the point.

Daily Inspirations From God's Word

April 15

This righteousness is given through faith in Jesus Christ to all who believe. There is no difference between Jew and Gentile, for all have sinned and fall short of the glory of God.

~ Romans 3:22-23 NIV

While the Jews were God's chosen people through which salvation would come, Jesus came to save people of all nations and to give his righteousness to all who believe.

April 16

That I may gain Christ and be found in him, not having a righteousness of my own that comes from the law, but that which is through faith in Christ—the righteousness that comes from God on the basis of faith. ~ Philippians 3:8b-9 NIV

Daily Inspirations From God's Word

It doesn't matter what family we were born into, the size of our bank account, or how much education we have.

No accomplishment, gold medal, or citizenship award merits anything apart from Christ. Knowing Him matters more than anything else.

April 17

God made him who had no sin to be sin for us, so that in him we might become the righteousness of God. ~ 2 Corinthians 5:21 NIV

Jesus—who is fully God and fully man—never sinned. Therefore, he was the only acceptable sacrifice able to pay for man's sin. We who believe in him by faith, receive his righteousness.

Daily Inspirations From God's Word

April 18

Christ is the culmination of the law so that there may be righteousness for everyone who believes. ~ Romans 10:4 NIV

Christ is the end of the law, which showed us our sin. No one but Christ, who is perfect, was able to keep the law. We do not receive righteousness by keeping a set of rules or doing any works. But, every sinner who believes by faith receives Christ's righteousness.

April 19

I delight greatly in the Lord; my soul rejoices in my God. For he has clothed me with garments of salvation and arrayed me in a robe of his righteousness. ~ Isaiah 61:10a NIV

Isaiah tells us later in his writings that our righteousness is like filthy rags (64:6). We cannot do anything to clean ourselves up. We cannot save ourselves. Apart from Christ, we could not come into the Father's presence. But Praise Jesus, he has taken our filthy garments and placed his garment of righteousness on us. Now we can come into the Father's presence – clean and made right!

April 20

You Lord are forgiving and good, abounding in love to all who call to you. ~ Psalm 86:5 NIV

You can always call on the Lord. Sometimes it is good to be reminded that he is good, he loves us, and he is always willing to forgive us.

April 21

But you, Lord, are a compassionate and gracious God, slow to anger, abounding in love and faithfulness. ~ Psalm 86:15 NIV

In a world where people are often unmerciful and rude, what a different world it would be if we followed God's example.

April 22

In you, Lord my God, I put my trust.

~Psalm 25:1 NIV

Some put their trust in money; some put their trust in people. But the one who puts his trust in the Lord will not be disappointed.

Daily Inspirations From God's Word

April 23

Hear my voice when I call, Lord; be merciful to me and answer me. My heart says of you, 'seek His face!' Your face, Lord, I will seek.

~ *Psalm 27:7-8 NIV*

God longs for us to call on him and seek His face. When we seek Him, we will find that He answers.

April24

When the wicked advance against me to devour me, it is my enemies and my foes who will stumble and fall. Though an army besiege me, my heart will not fear; though war break out against me, even then I will be confident.

~ *Psalm 27:2-3 NIV*

In the unseen world as well as the natural, physical world, things or people may come against us. Like the psalmist, we can only remain confident if we know whose we are. Therefore, we need not fear the army or the war.

April 25

For in the day of trouble He will keep me safe in His dwelling. He will hide me in the shelter of His sacred tent and set me high upon a rock.

~ Psalm 27:5 NIV

Though trouble may assail us, faith believes in the One who is able to keep us safe in His presence. In Christ we are hidden in Him, and He lifts us up.

Daily Inspirations From God's Word

April 26

I will remain confident of this: I will see the goodness of the Lord in the land of the living. Wait for the Lord; be strong and take heart and wait for the Lord. ~ Psalm 27:13-14 NIV

Like David, our confidence should be in God. David knew God's goodness and believed he would see it in this life, while he waited on him in faith. Waiting for God can seem hard, but often God is teaching us during this time. What we do in the waiting period is important. We must be strong in the waiting and stay focused on His promises.

April 27

Enter His gates with thanksgiving and His courts with Praise; give thanks to Him and praise His name. ~ Psalm 100:4 NIV

Daily Inspirations From God's Word

Like all kingdoms, God's kingdom has a throne. When we enter a King's presence, we approach him with reverence and praise. Through prayer, visualize entering through the gates with a grateful heart of praise for our Lord and King. All prayer starts not with requests, but with praise and thanksgiving.

April 28

Let us come before Him with Thanksgiving and extol Him with music and song.

~ Psalm 95:2 NIV

We express our thankfulness through worship for what God has done for us. The more we realize the many times He has rescued and helped us, the more our hearts will want to express our gratitude

Daily Inspirations From God's Word

April 29

Do not be anxious for anything, but in everything, by prayer and petition, with thanksgiving, present your requests to God.

~ Philippians 4:6 NIV

Anxiety will attack us from time to time. When we take God at his Word, we bring to him everything that makes us anxious. During those times God tells us to come to him by praying with a thankful heart. Tell him everything and receive his peace.

April 30

Give thanks in all circumstances.

~ 1 Thessalonians 5:18 NIV

Death of a loved one, a job loss, a car wreck, financial loss, or any setback are circumstances that cause us grief rather than

Daily Inspirations From God's Word

thankfulness. It takes faith to give thanks in such circumstances. We may not understand the why at the moment, but God does. If we look beyond the situation, we can believe that God will bring good in all of them. We can be thankful for the loved one's life, though we feel the pain of loss. We can be thankful for the next opportunity that a job loss brings. A car wreck can end up being a lesson we needed. Even in financial loss, we can be thankful that God will sustain us as we learn to depend on Him.

May 1

But thanks be to God, who always leads us in triumphal procession in Christ and through us spreads everywhere the fragrance of the knowledge of Him. ~ 2 Corinthians 2:14 NIV

Daily Inspirations From God's Word

What an honor to be led by God and used by God as an aroma of Him in the lives of others. Are you thankful when God uses you?

May 2

Give thanks to the Lord, call on His name; make known among the nations what He has done.

~ 1 Chronicles 16:8 NIV

This is the first verse of David's psalm of thanks to the Lord after the people of Israel brought the ark of God to Jerusalem. Do you remember a time God showed His faithfulness to you? Your heart rejoiced in thankfulness at His love and care for you and you wanted to make it known.

May 3

So then, just as you received Christ Jesus as Lord, continue to live in Him, rooted and built up in Him, strengthened in the faith as you were taught, and overflowing with thankfulness.

~ Colossians 2:6-7 NIV

Once we receive Christ, our faith will grow as we continue to learn of Him. In a similar way that a new seedling grows into a plant by developing a root system, we grow in Jesus. The one who cares for the plant nourishes it by feeding and watering it so it grows strong. A plant does not gain strength unless it is firmly rooted. By feeding on God's Word and living in Him we will mature. As we live in Him and are united with Him, we overflow with thankfulness.

Daily Inspirations From God's Word

May 4

For everything that was written in the past was written to teach us, so that through endurance and encouragement of the scriptures we might have hope. ~ Romans 15:4 NIV

People who regularly read God's Word receive the blessing of wisdom and encouragement. History shows us the lives of those who failed, overcame hardships, and persevered to victory. We learn to endure by watching those who endured and we gain encouragement and hope for our own lives.

May 5

May the God who gives endurance and encouragement give you a spirit of unity among yourselves as you follow Christ Jesus.

~ Romans 15:5 NIV

Daily Inspirations From God's Word

We live in a diverse world. We often find ourselves surrounded by people different from us—in their viewpoints, style of worship or communication. As we follow Christ in our walk, when we ask Him, He will give us a spirit of unity just as He gives endurance and encouragement.

May 6

If we are distressed, it is for your comfort and salvation; if we are comforted, it is for your comfort, which produces in you patient endurance of the same sufferings we suffer.

> *~ 2 Corinthians 1:6 NIV*

We often recoil from suffering. Christ suffered on our behalf. When we suffer, it draws us closer to Him. Suffering causes spiritual growth, produces perseverance, and helps us to encourage others who suffer.

Daily Inspirations From God's Word

May 7

Rather, as servants of God we commend ourselves in every way: in great endurance; in troubles, hardships and distresses; in beatings, imprisonments and riots; in hard work, sleepless nights and hunger.

~ 2 Corinthians 6:4-5 NIV

Suffering comes into every life. How we react to it is important. We can let any difficult situation harden our heart and cause us to become bitter. Or we can decide to allow God to use it for good. When others see in us the hope we have despite our circumstances, it reflects what and Who we believe in.

May 8

...being strengthened with all power according to His glorious might so that you may have great endurance and patience. ~ Colossians 1:11 NIV

Daily Inspirations From God's Word

It is the Spirit who gives strength and power. It is the Spirit who enables us to have great endurance and patience according to His glorious might. Pray in the Spirit for these things.

May 9

We continually remember before our God and Father your work produced by faith, your labor prompted by love, and your endurance inspired by hope in our Lord Jesus Christ.

~1 Thessalonians 1:3 NIV

People will remember us for many different things. Will you be remembered for any of these? Ask Christ to cultivate these characteristics in you.

Daily Inspirations From God's Word

May 10

For the love of money is a root of all kinds of evil. Some people, eager for money, have wandered from the faith and pierced themselves with many griefs. But you man of God, flee from all this, and pursue righteousness, godliness, faith, love, endurance and gentleness.

~1 Timothy 6:10-11 NIV

Money in itself is not a bad thing. The scripture says the love of money is. Therefore, we are not to always seek after it but are to grow in contentment. We are to help others by sharing the money we have. When we actively pursue living godly, we will find great joy.

May 11

Be strong and courageous, because you will lead these people to inherit the land I swore to their forefathers to give them. ~ Joshua 1:6 NIV

Daily Inspirations From God's Word

After Moses died, Joshua had the difficult job of taking his place to lead the Israelites into the promised land. Like Joshua, we may find ourselves in a leadership position, following in the footsteps of someone great. In those moments it's easy to fear and question the call. But we can take these words the Lord spoke to Joshua for ourselves. "Be strong and courageous because you will lead these people..." maybe not to the promised land, perhaps to the next level, perhaps in a new direction. As the new leader you have benefited from the one before you. You were placed in this leadership position because you are qualified. So "be strong and courageous!"

May 12

Amariah the chief priest will be over you in any matter concerning the LORD, and Zebadiah son of Ishmael, the leader of the tribe of Judah, will be over you in any matter concerning the king, and the Levites will serve as officials before you. Act with courage, and may the LORD be with those who do well. ~ *2 Chronicles 19:11 NIV*

King Jehoshaphat of Jerusalem appointed judges over the people. He also appointed the Levite priests to administer the law of the LORD and to settle disputes among them. As in Jehoshaphat's day, those in charge of different ranks are accountable to the people over them. When in charge, a leader must act with courage.

May 13

But when they saw him (Jesus) walking on the lake, they thought he was a ghost. They cried out, because they all saw him and were terrified. Immediately he spoke to them and said, 'Take courage! It is I. Don't be afraid.'

~ *Mark 6:49-50 NIV*

Daily Inspirations From God's Word

This event occurred after the disciples witnessed the feeding of the five thousand. Afterward, Jesus sent them off in a boat away from the crowds. They had rowed all night. Jesus walked out to them when he saw they were in trouble, straining against the wind. They were terrified. In the midst of our "deep water" problems that terrify us, we can forget that Jesus is right there. We can take courage, because He is with us.

May 14

When they saw the courage of Peter and John and realized that they were unschooled, ordinary men, they were astonished and they took note that these men had been with Jesus.

~Acts 4:13 NIV

After his arrest, all of the disciples deserted Jesus, just as he said they would. But after the coming of the Holy Spirit on Pentecost, these were noticeably different men. Now filled with the Holy Spirit, boldness and courage filled them. We are filled with the Spirit at the moment of salvation. Like Peter and John, we as ordinary people can overflow with boldness and courage to speak our faith.

May 15

So keep up your courage men, for I have faith in God that it will happen just as He told me.

~ Act 27:25 NIV

Paul—a prisoner on board a ship during a raging storm—encourages the crew! We may not have an angel of the Lord appear to us as he did. But Paul had to have faith in what God told him. Paul serves as an example to us as we strive to keep our courage and faith in the midst of trials we face.

Daily Inspirations From God's Word

May 16

Be on your guard; stand firm in the faith; be men of courage; be strong. ~ 1 Corinthians 16:13 NIV

These are wise instructions that Paul left for the Corinthians as they awaited his return. In our world today, we need to be on guard against evil and stand firm in our faith. We should know what we believe, take courage, and be fearless and strong.

May 17

But Christ is faithful as a son over God's house. And we are his house, if we hold on to our courage and the hope of which we boast.

~ Hebrews 3:6 NIV

Courage and hope reveal the genuineness of our faith. Holding on to them takes endurance and persistence. Without this enduring faithfulness, we can easily be swayed by all kinds of temptations and false teaching. By holding fast to our faith, our house is built up not swayed.

May 18

So David went up in obedience to the word that Gad had spoken in the name of the LORD.
~1 Chronicles 21:19 NIV

In the preceding verses, (1Chronicles 21:1-18), David conducted a census which God had not commanded, and this sin caused seventy-thousand innocent people to die. Our sin affects not only us, but others as well.

When David went up in obedience, it was to build an altar to the Lord at his command. What great sin is God asking you to take responsibility for and turn back in obedience to him?

Daily Inspirations From God's Word

May 19

He who obeys instructions guards his life, but he who is contemptuous of his ways will die.

> *~Proverbs 19:16 NIV*

The favor of the Lord rests upon those who obey Him. But those who refuse in arrogance end in self-destruction. God has given us His Spirit to help us obey Him because He wants us to live in His favor.

May 20

This service that you perform is not only supplying the needs of the Lord's people but is also overflowing in many expressions of thanks to God. Because of the service by which you have proved yourselves, men will praise God for obedience that accompanies your confession of the gospel of Christ, and for your generosity in

Daily Inspirations From God's Word

sharing with them and with everyone else.
                    ~2 Corinthians 9:13 NIV

We've all seen reports of hurricanes or tornadoes and the devastation they leave behind. The plight of families left with nothing and in need of everything overwhelms us. We're all called to share what we have and to give sacrificially. When we give generously, the expression of thanks on a needy person's face brings us deep joy.

May 21

Whoever has my commands and obeys them, he is the one who loves me. He who loves me will be loved by my Father, and I too will love him and show myself to him. ~ John 14:21 NIV

As Jesus' followers we show our love for Him by obeying Him, not only in lip service, but also in our commitment and conduct. We prove our love for Him by our actions.

May 22

Although he was a son, he learned obedience from what he suffered and, once made perfect, he became the source of eternal salvation for all who obey him. ~ Hebrews 5:8 NIV

When we study Jesus' prayer in the Garden of Gethsemane, we clearly see the struggle he felt as he asked the Father to remove the cup he was about to drink. He knew the agony that lay ahead, not only physically—great as that was—but mentally, emotionally and spiritually. Jesus took the sin of mankind upon himself. Jesus chose to obey. He willingly went to the cross, preferring not his will but the Father's. Eternal death was defeated because of his obedience. Praise his holy name!

May 23

But I gave them this command: Obey me, and I will be your God and you will be my people. Walk in all the ways I command you, that it may go well with you. But they did not listen or pay attention; instead, they followed the stubborn inclinations of their evil hearts. They went backward and not forward.

~ *Jeremiah 7:23-24 NIV*

The prophet Jeremiah reminded the people of Judah what God had said long ago to the children of Israel when He brought them out of Egypt. Like their forefathers, the people of Judah would disobey God's commands. God gives us many chances to respond to correction. We see many people today going backward and not forward. If we want the

Daily Inspirations From God's Word

blessing of God on our lives and our families we will walk in His ways and teach others to do the same!

May 24

Teach me, O LORD, to follow your decrees; then I will keep them to the end. Give me understanding, and I will keep your law and obey it with all my heart. Direct me in the path of your commands, for there I find delight.

~Psalm 119:33-35 NIV

Like the psalmist's prayer, we can ask God to teach us how to follow Him. We can ask God for understanding about His Word so that we know what it says. And we can ask God to direct our path to His commands. God loves to answer prayers like that because He desires us to know Him and His ways.

May 25

A man's wisdom gives him patience; it is to his glory to overlook an offense.

~ Proverbs 19:11 NIV

Time and experience teach us to be sensible and self-controlled – in some cases – the hard way. Sometimes the hardest thing is to overlook an offense, but by doing so, we earn respect.

May 26

A patient man has great understanding but a quick-tempered man displays folly.

~Proverbs 14:29 NIV

We are able to control anger when we begin to understand the harm it causes in relationships. Those who are quick to lose it show foolishness.

Daily Inspirations From God's Word

May 27

Be joyful in hope, patient in affliction, faithful in prayer. ~ Romans 12:12 NIV

Although it's easy to lose hope, to despair over affliction, and to cease praying. If we are to live victoriously, we need help from God. Faithful prayer must be the key.

May 28

Be still before the LORD and wait patiently for him; do not fret when men succeed in their ways, when they carry out their wicked schemes.

~ Psalm 37:7 NIV

The practice of being still before the Lord, even for a few moments each day, increases our awareness of His presence. Although the wait seems long, God will act in His way and in His time. Even when those who do wrong appear to be getting away with their deeds, God sees.

May 29

The Lord is not slow in keeping his promise, as some understand slowness. He is patient with you, not wanting anyone to perish, but everyone to come to repentance. ~ 2 Peter 3:9 NIV

We all have a long list of people who have not acknowledged the Lord as Savior in their life. I am thankful that God patiently waits for people to turn to Him before He comes back. When Jesus comes back, no one can say God didn't give people plenty of time to turn away from wrongdoing.

May 30

Be patient, then, brothers, until the Lord's coming. See how the farmer waits for the land to yield its valuable crop and how patient he is for the autumn and spring rains. You too, be patient and stand firm, because the Lord's coming is near. ~ James 5:7-8 NIV

Many people find it hard to wait. When someone we love says they are coming to see us, we can hardly wait until that day. James encourages us to be patient, like a farmer who waits for a return on his hard work. He can do nothing to hurry the rains that will help his crop grow. We too, must be patient and not give up. The Lord's return could be nearer than we think.

May 31

And we urge you, brothers, warn those who are idle, encourage the timid, help the weak, be patient with everyone.

~1 Thessalonians 5:14 NIV

Daily Inspirations From God's Word

Do you know some lazy people? Warn them, Paul instructs. Do you know fearful people? Encourage them. Do you pass by weak people, or do you help them? We encounter many people who try our patience. We can be an example to others and display patience toward them. Someday we may find we need the same for ourselves.

June 1

For the LORD your God is a merciful God; he will not abandon or destroy you or forget the covenant with your forefathers, which he confirmed to them by oath.

~ Deuteronomy 4:31 NIV

Over and over the children of Israel had rebelled against the Lord. Moses reminded them if they return to the Lord, He is merciful. The same is true when we rebel and go our own way. If we turn to the Lord and come back, He is merciful and will forgive us.

June 2

Be merciful to those who doubt; snatch others from the fire and save them; to others show mercy, mixed with fear – hating even the clothing stained by corrupted flesh.

~ Jude 22 NIV

We meet many people who do not believe in Jesus. We show mercy to them and rescue them from coming judgment when we share our faith. We hate the sin, but love the sinner.

June 3

For many years you were patient with them. By

your Spirit you admonished them through your prophets. Yet they paid no attention, so you handed them over to the neighboring peoples. But in your great mercy you did not put an end to them or abandon them, for you are a gracious and merciful God. ~ Nehemiah 9:31 NIV

History is a great teacher. Israel's past helps us to see the depth of God's love for them. The people of Israel paid no attention to the warnings God sent them. As many children do, they insisted in their way, and ended up experiencing the consequences for their actions. A wise person will learn from their example, and also be gracious and merciful to those under them, as God is with us.

June 4

Hear my cry for mercy as I call to you for help, as I lift up my hands toward your Most Holy Place.

Daily Inspirations From God's Word

Praise be to the LORD, for He has heard my cry for mercy. ~ Psalm 28:2 & 6 NIV

Have you ever found yourself surrounded by trouble, or devious people trying to do you wrong? Call to God, who is our only help when faced with trials. You will find He gives wisdom, provides a way out, and shelters you with His Mighty Hand. Then like David, you will add your thanks and praise for answering your cry for mercy.

June 5

He who conceals his sins does not prosper, but whoever confesses and renounces them finds mercy. ~ Proverbs 28:13 NIV

As a child did you ever break something valuable, and then try to hide it? It is natural to try to hide our sin, or look the other way on our mistakes. Adam and Eve did that too. We try to cover because we have guilt. Rather than covering up, God's way is different. He calls us to confess it and bring it into the open before Him. Then we find His mercy which frees us from the guilt and shame.

June 6

But because of His great love for us, God, who is rich in mercy, made us alive with Christ even when we were dead in transgressions – it is by grace you have been saved.

~ Ephesians 2:4-5 NIV

Before we trust Jesus, sin wields enormous power over us. Yet we see that while we were dead in transgressions, Jesus broke the power of sin and made us alive with him – all because of God's great love and mercy for us. Our salvation is a gift of God's grace when we place our faith in Him.

June 7

I thank Christ Jesus our Lord, who has given me strength, that He considered me faithful, appointing me to His service. Even though I was once a blasphemer and a persecutor and a violent man, I was shown mercy because I acted in ignorance and unbelief.

~ 1 Timothy 1:12-13 NIV

Because of what we've done in the past, we think God could never use us. But Paul was an educated man, a Pharisee himself, who had Christians arrested and put to death because he was ignorant of the truth. God can turn the coldest, hardest heart, show them mercy, and greatly use them once they've been transformed by Christ.

June 8

He holds victory in store for the upright, he is a shield to those whose walk is blameless, for he guards the course of the just and protects the way of his faithful ones. ~ Proverbs 2:7-8 NIV

Many people disregard God and the teachings in the Bible. When we walk according to God's ways, the Bible teaches that God blesses by shielding and protecting his faithful ones.

June 9

It was the LORD our God himself who brought us and our fathers up out of Egypt, from that land of slavery, and performed those great signs before our eyes. He protected us on our entire journey and among all the nations through which we traveled. ~ Joshua 24:17 NIV

For 400 years, the Israelites had been enslaved in Egypt. God used Moses to deliver the people out of bondage into unknown territory. God protected the people from the beginning of their journey to the end. God is faithful. We are not guaranteed a problem-free life, but faith places trust in God no matter what the outcome.

June 10

May integrity and uprightness protect me, because my hope, LORD, is in you.

~ Psalm 25:21 NIV

It is not the wicked, deceitful people who can hope to find protection, but those who live honest lives.

Daily Inspirations From God's Word

June 11

You are my hiding place; you will protect me from trouble and surround me with songs of deliverance. ~ Psalm 32:7 NIV

Have you ever hidden where no one could find you? In the unseen world, we make God our hiding place. When we call on Him, God offers protection, and He surrounds us with songs of victory.

June 12

If you say, 'The LORD is my refuge,' and you make the Most High your dwelling, no harm will overtake you, no disaster will come near your tent. 'Because he loves me,' says the LORD, 'I will rescue him; I will protect him, for he acknowledges my name.'

~ Psalm 91:9-10, 14 NIV

We live in a dangerous world. God doesn't

promise us that we will never face danger, but He does promise to help us. When you are afraid, call upon the Lord. He is your refuge, dwell with Him. Love the Lord, acknowledge His name, and He will rescue you.

June 13

My prayer is not that you take them out of the world but that you protect them from the evil one. ~John 17:15 NIV

Jesus knew we would have trouble in this world so He prayed that God would protect us from the devil. God doesn't remove us from trouble; He protects and enables us while we go through it.

Daily Inspirations From God's Word

June 14

Rescue me, LORD, from evildoers; protect me from the violent, who devise their plans in their hearts and stir up war every day. Keep me safe, LORD, from the hands of the wicked; protect me from the violent, who devise ways to trip my feet. The arrogant have hidden a snare for me; they have spread out the cords of their net and have set traps for me along my path. Sovereign LORD, you shield me in the day of battle.

~ Psalm 140: 1-2, 4-5,7. NIV

David prayed often for protection from pursuers. We also need to pray for ourselves, for protection from those who seek to harm us. God is our shield in the day of battle.

June 15

And you, my son Solomon, acknowledge the God of your father, and serve him with wholehearted

Daily Inspirations From God's Word

devotion and with a willing mind, for the LORD sees every motive behind the thoughts. If you seek him, he will be found by you; but if you forsake him, he will reject you forever.

~ 1 Chronicles 28:9 NIV

David instructed his son Solomon, the one chosen to build the temple for the ark of the Lord. But David's advice is for us, too. Since God knows our hearts and our motives, we would be wise to serve him wholeheartedly. He knows the best and the worst about us. And He loves us still.

June 16

The LORD looks down from heaven on the sons of men to see if there are any who understand, any who seek God. ~ Psalm 14:2 NIV

Are you seeking Him? Do you want him to

recognize you as one who does, among so many who do not? We may not understand everything, but when we seek God, asking Him for understanding, He will give it.

June 17

And He said to man, 'The fear of the LORD — that is wisdom, and to shun evil is understanding. ~ Job 28:28 NIV

God hates evil. If we love God, we will hate evil, too. When we grasp how much God detests it, we will avoid even the appearance of evil.

June 18

My son, if you accept my words and store up my commands within you, turning your ear to wisdom and applying your heart to understanding, and if you call out for insight and cry aloud for understanding, and if you look for it as for silver and search for it as for hidden treasure, then you will understand the fear of the LORD and find the knowledge of God.

~ Proverbs 2:1-5NIV

Wisdom and the fear of the LORD go hand and hand with understanding. As the Creator of Heaven and earth, God is in control of all things. When we understand this, and believe his love for us, then we will have "the fear of the LORD." God reveals himself to earnest seekers.

June 19

Trust in the LORD with all your heart and lean not on your own understanding.

~ Proverbs 3:5 NIV

Daily Inspirations From God's Word

When we try to figure things out on our own apart from God, we find they don't turn out well. That is why the writer of Proverbs instructs us to trust in the LORD. Trusting God takes faith. Trusting God takes us from self-reliance to dependence on Him. God can be trusted with every decision, because He is faithful and knows what is best for us.

June 20

Blessed is the man who finds wisdom, the man who gains understanding, for she is more profitable than silver and yields better returns than gold. ~ Proverbs 3:13-14 NIV

The man who doesn't find wisdom and understanding is a poor man indeed. The benefits of wisdom and understanding lead us to right choices.

Daily Inspirations From God's Word

June 21

We know also that the Son of God has come and has given us understanding, so that we may know Him who is true. And we are in Him who is true – by being in His Son Jesus Christ. He is the true God and eternal life. ~ 1 John 5:20 NIV

Jesus came to give us understanding so that we could know God. Because Jesus and God are one, we who belong to Christ, belong to the Father who gives eternal life.

June 22

For the eyes of the LORD range throughout the earth to strengthen those whose hearts are fully committed to Him. You have done a foolish thing, and from now on you will be at war.

~ 2Chronicles 16:9 NIV

The above quote is an admonishment to King

Asa of Judah by Hanani the seer. King Asa took the silver and gold out of the treasuries of the LORD's temple, then he gave them to the King of Aram to make a treaty with him. Rather than trust God, King Asa sought help from a pagan king. People do foolish things, forgetting that God sees everything. He knows when our hearts are fully committed to Him and He knows when they are not. There will always be consequences for our wrong actions.

June 23

My eyes are ever on the LORD, for only He will release my feet from the snare.

~ Psalm 25:15 NIV

When we turn to God, trusting only Him, we become certain that He is the only one who is able to rescue us.

Daily Inspirations From God's Word

June 24

Turn my eyes away from worthless things;
preserve my life according to your Word.

~ Psalm 119:37 NIV

Many meaningless things that have no eternal
value vie for our attention. We can pray that
God will turn our eyes away from such things,
preserve, and protect us from the world's
contamination.

June 25

My frame was not hidden from You when I was
made in the secret place. When I was woven
together in the depths of the earth, your eyes saw
my unformed body. All the days ordained for me
were written in your book before one of them
came to be. ~ Psalm 139:15-16 NIV

How amazing to think that God knew us even
before he formed us. Our Creator God is

omnipresent. He is unlimited by time and space and He alone knows all of our days. He knows the beginning and the end.

June 26

So we fix our eyes not on what is seen, but on what is unseen. For what is seen is temporary, but what is unseen is eternal.

~ 2Corinthians 4:18 NIV

If all we see is trouble in this life, we must remember it is temporary. This life is not all there is. There is another life to come – after death. Grasping the unseen that is yet to come can help us cope with the troubles we face now.

Daily Inspirations From God's Word

June 27

I pray also that the eyes of your heart may be enlightened in order that you may know the hope to which He has called you, the riches of His glorious inheritance in the saints.

~ Ephesians 1:18 NIV

We can know with certainty that God has called us to something beyond anything this world can offer; the riches of God's inheritance to us who believe.

June 28

Let us fix our eyes on Jesus, the author and perfecter of our faith, who for the joy set before Him endured the cross, scorning its shame, and sat down at the right hand of the throne of God.

~ Hebrews 12:2 NIV

Daily Inspirations From God's Word

So many people give up and quit when life gets hard. For the believer, Jesus is our example and we overcome when we keep our eyes on Him. He is the One who perfects our faith as we grow. He victoriously endured the cross to the end because He knew the end result was our freedom – our salvation. Don't lose sight of Jesus when it gets tough.

June 29

May your unfailing love come to me, O LORD, your salvation according to your promise. I will walk about in freedom, for I have sought out your precepts. ~ Psalm 119:41,45 NIV

Seeking salvation from God frees us from the power of sin and death. We are unrestrained when we walk according to God's ways; we become free to be the person he meant us to be.

Daily Inspirations From God's Word

June 30

But whenever anyone turns to the Lord, the veil is taken away. Now the Lord is the Spirit, and where the Spirit of the Lord is, there is freedom.

~ *2Corinthians 3:16-17 NIV*

God gave Moses the Ten Commandments on Mt. Sinai. Because Moses had been in God's presence, his face radiated brilliant light. The people were afraid of his glowing face, so he wore a veil. The veil also represented the people's minds. Their understanding was veiled because of sin and unrepentant hearts. When we turn to Christ for salvation, the veil is removed. God reveals truth to us and gives us understanding. We are free from the burden of trying to keep the law because God's Spirit now lives in us.

Daily Inspirations From God's Word

July 1

It is for freedom that Christ has set us free. Stand firm, then, and do not let yourselves be burdened again by a yoke of slavery. ~ Galatians 5:1 NIV

In addition to the law, God gave Moses, the religious leaders added many rules of their own. Jesus came and fulfilled the law, freeing us from the burden of trying to keep it. Though we are free, we are not to slip back into sin by the selfish desires of our heart. Neither are we to fall into the practice of keeping rules and methods imposed by others.

July 2

Do not merely listen to the word, and so deceive yourselves. Do what it says. But the man who looks intently into the perfect law that gives freedom, and continues to do this, not forgetting

*what he has heard, but doing it – he will be
blessed in what he does. ~ James 1:22,25 NIV*

Many people attend church and listen to the
teaching of the word, but people also leave
church and fall into the same habits. Some
argue with family, some curse in traffic, some
gossip – unchanged by the very words they
heard. James is saying, "do not be deceived by
just listening." We are to purpose in our hearts
to live in obedience to the word. That is where
we find freedom.

July 3

*Live as free men, but do not use your freedom as
a cover-up for evil; live as servants of God.*

~ 1Peter 2:16 NIV

Christians are free from the rules of religious
law and legalism, but we are not to abuse our
freedom. God places laws in the government
that are his will for us to follow. One example

we see in society is when people make excuses for not paying taxes, pay taxes late, or cheat on taxes and think nothing is wrong with that. In *Matthew 22:15-21,* when asked about paying taxes to Caesar, the Lord Jesus said, *'Give to Caesar what is Caesar's, and to God what is God's.'*

July 4

The Spirit of the Sovereign LORD is on me, because the LORD has anointed me to preach good news to the poor. He has sent me to bind up the brokenhearted, to proclaim freedom for the captives and release from darkness the prisoners. ~Isaiah 61:1 NIV

Isaiah prophesied these words and Jesus quoted them about himself in Luke 4:18. Sin places us in bondage. We are spiritual captives of the evil one and we remain in darkness until Christ comes into our lives. The preaching of the good news is all about Jesus, who is the One God anointed and sent to release the spiritual prisoner to set him free from sin.

July 5

To Him who loves us and has freed us from our sins by his blood, and has made us to be a kingdom and priests to serve His God and Father – to Him be glory and power forever! Amen.

~ Revelation 1:5b-6 NIV

Jesus loved us so much, it took His blood shed on the cross to free us from our sin. We who believe and have been freed are now citizens of the kingdom of Heaven. God has made us priests, which gives us the opportunity to minister God's love to others. This is how we serve our Father in Heaven.

Daily Inspirations From God's Word

July 6

So Samuel took the horn of oil and anointed him in the presence of his brothers, and from that day on the Spirit of the LORD came upon David in power. ~ 1Samuel 16:13 NIV

David was a young shepherd when Samuel anointed him. The anointing of oil represents holiness, and set David apart for God's service. When we receive the Holy Spirit at the time of our salvation, we too are set apart. We now have the power of the Spirit within us to serve God.

July 7

Be strong and courageous. Do not be afraid or discouraged because of the king of Assyria and the vast army with him, for there is a greater power with us than with him. With him is only the arm of flesh, but with us is the LORD our God

Daily Inspirations From God's Word

to help us and to fight our battles.

~ 2Chronicles 32:7-8 NIV

When Sennacherib king of Assyria invaded Judah and laid siege to the fortified cities, Hezekiah acted quickly. He reinforced and repaired city walls, and built large numbers of weapons. Then Hezekiah summoned the military officers and reminded the people that they had God's power on their side. When we face difficult and dangerous situations, we do what we can to resolve the problem while trusting God for the outcome.

July 8

Jotham grew powerful because he walked steadfastly before the LORD his God.

~ 2 Chronicles 27:6 NIV

Jotham was twenty-five when he became king

of Jerusalem. Not all kings did what was right in the eyes of the Lord, but Jotham did. He is an example that shows God rewards steadfast obedience.

July 9

So he said to me, 'This is the word of the LORD to Zerubbabel: Not by might nor by my power, but by my Spirit,' says the LORD Almighty.

~ Zechariah 4:6 NIV

We accomplish nothing of eternal value in our own strength. We must trust not in ourselves, but in God's Spirit alone who empowers us.

July 10

But you will receive power when the Holy Spirit comes on you; and you will be my witnesses in

Daily Inspirations From God's Word

Jerusalem, and in all Judea and Samaria, and to the ends of the earth. ~ Acts 1:8 NIV

When you believe in Jesus Christ, you receive the Holy Spirit, and the power to reach others for Christ. His power includes the boldness to witness for him with courage, and confidence to speak up. The Holy Spirit enables the believer to spread the gospel and be God's witness throughout the world.

July 11

For the Scripture says to Pharaoh: 'I raised you up for this very purpose, that I might display my power in you and that my name might be proclaimed in all the earth. ~ Romans 9:17 NIV

God can display his power through anybody, including bad guys. In the great Exodus, God displayed many miracles (ten plagues) when

Daily Inspirations From God's Word

Pharaoh refused to let the people go. God also gave Pharaoh many chances to soften his heart, but he refused. In the end, Israel's great escape from Egypt displayed God's great and mighty power. Could the trials in our lives be used by God to cause us to cry out? When all goes well, we have no need to call on God. But when life presses or someone mistreats us, we become desperate for God. He may take a long time to deliver us, but when he does, his power and glory is revealed.

July 12

I am not ashamed of the gospel, because it is the power of God for the salvation of everyone who believes: first for the Jew, then for the Gentile.

~ Romans 1:16 NIV

Have you ever been embarrassed or ashamed to share the gospel because you didn't know

Daily Inspirations From God's Word

how? We need not be ashamed to share the good news of the gospel because its message is simple. Christ died on the cross in our place to pay the penalty for mankind's sin. The power of God rose him up from the grave, giving victory over death. Those who believe in Jesus will live forever with him in Heaven and be saved from hell. Helping people find life in Christ is a wonderful motivation for overcoming the fear of sharing.

July 13

And now, O Israel, what does the LORD your God ask of you but to fear the LORD your God, to walk in all his ways, to love him, to serve the LORD your God with all your heart and with all your soul. ~ Deuteronomy 10:12 NIV

Moses instructed the people in what the Lord expected of them. When we fear the Lord, it is a reverential fear. When we walk in all his ways, we are obeying. We are to love him and serve him with all that is in us.

July 14
And Samuel said to the whole house of Israel, 'If you are returning to the LORD with all your hearts, then rid yourselves of the foreign gods and the Ashtoreths and commit yourselves to the LORD and serve him only, and he will deliver you out of the hand of the Philistines.

~ 1Samuel 7:3 NIV

An idol is anything that controls us and takes the place of God in our lives. It does not have to be a wooden object. It can be money, lust for power, success, pride or, anything else that rivals God's place. When we commit ourselves to the Lord and serve him only, he will bless us.

Daily Inspirations From God's Word

July 15

If we are thrown into the blazing furnace, the God we serve is able to save us from it, and he will rescue us from your hand, O king.

~ Daniel 3:17 NIV

Shadrach, Meshach, and Abednego trusted in God and chose not to bow down to Nebuchadnezzar's idol. They were willing to give up their lives rather than serve and worship an idol. They took a stand and didn't compromise their convictions even though it could have cost them their lives. It may not always end that way, but the Christian should be prepared to say, "If God rescues me or not I will only serve him.

July 16

Again, the devil took him to a very high mountain and showed him all the kingdoms of the world

Daily Inspirations From God's Word

and their splendor. 'All this I will give you,' he said, 'if you will bow down and worship me.' Jesus said to him, 'away from me, Satan! For it is written: 'Worship the Lord your God, and serve him only.' ~ Matthew 4:8-10 NIV

We will be tempted many times by the devil, but Jesus gives us a powerful example to follow. Rebuke the devil, quote God's Word, and refuse to give into the devil's demands to worship and serve him. When we love God, our heart will worship and serve Him only.

July 17

Serve wholeheartedly, as if you were serving the Lord, not men, because you know that the Lord will reward everyone for whatever good he does, whether he is free or slave. ~ Ephesians 6:7 NIV

Often people grow weary of serving others.

Daily Inspirations From God's Word

Our perspective can change when we remember that serving others pleases God and is really serving him.

July 18

Each one should use whatever gift he has received to serve others, faithfully administering God's grace in various forms. ~ 1Peter 4:10 NIV

We have all been given gifts with which we can use to serve others. The body of believers can meet the various needs within the church. Some can sing, some play a musical instrument, other have gifts of administration, leadership, or teaching. Others are creative. Whatever your gift use it faithfully to serve others.

Daily Inspirations From God's Word

July 19

Jesus called them together and said, 'You know that the rulers of the Gentiles lord it over them, and their high officials exercise authority over them. Not so with you. Instead, whoever wants to become great among you must be your servant, and whoever wants to be first must be your slave – just as the Son of Man did not come to be served, but to serve, and to give his life as a ransom for many.' ~ Matthew 20:25-28 NIV

Many people would like to have first place or be given highest honor among their peers. But Jesus told his disciples, "Whoever wants that place of greatness must be a servant to all." We can all be useful to God, but those who are most useful are God's humble servants.

July 20

They are always generous and lend freely; their children will be blessed. ~ Psalm 37:26 NIV

Daily Inspirations From God's Word

Those who belong to God will be generous out of love for him. Families who give willingly experience the outpouring of the Father's blessings.

July 21

Good will come to him who lends freely, who conducts his affairs with justice.

~ Psalm 112:5 NIV

Great wealth has the potential to bring blessing; it can also cause people to mistreat others. The love of money corrupts causing people to go to great lengths to keep from losing their money. But those who give generously out of respect and love for God will experience blessings.

Daily Inspirations From God's Word

July 22

One person gives freely, yet gains even more; another withholds unduly, but comes to poverty. A generous man will prosper; he who refreshes others will himself be refreshed.

~ Proverbs 11:24-25 NIV

We will never gain more by holding back. Those who realize everything they have comes from God, know that He blesses generous giving. This in turn leads to their ability to give to others out of their abundance. When we give to others, God will always give back to us.

July 23

Don't I have the right to do what I want with my own money? Or are you envious because I am generous? ~ Matthew 20:15 NIV

Daily Inspirations From God's Word

Jesus tells the parable of the vineyard workers. A land owner hired some men to work. Some men started early in the morning and some started late in the afternoon. The landowner paid them all the same. When the early workers heard of this, they complained. Jesus was speaking to the people who perhaps feel superior to others for all the work they've done for the Lord.

Do you know someone who accepted Christ at the end of a long life? They will be in heaven, the same as the person who was saved early in life and served God their whole life. It's by God's grace that we are saved, not through works.

July 24

We want you to know about the grace that God has given the Macedonian churches. Out of the most severe trial, their overflowing joy and their

extreme poverty welled up in rich generosity.
~ 2 Corinthians 8:1-2 NIV

One can be very poor but rich toward God, as were the Macedonian churches. In this case, these churches wanted to give, and they did so sacrificially. They were dedicated to Christ and wanted to show their love to Him and fellow believers who were also in need. Our giving shows an attitude of our heart toward God and others.

July 25

Remember this: Whoever sows sparingly will also reap sparingly, and whoever sows generously will also reap generously.
~ 2Corinthians 9:6 NIV

People sometimes hold back from giving generously because they may not see how their own needs will be met. But God sees, and

Daily Inspirations From God's Word

He knows when someone has given beyond their means. If we have faith to believe that we cannot out give God, then we will sow generously not sparingly.

July 26

Command them to do good, to be rich in good deeds, and to be generous and willing to share. In this way they will lay up treasure for themselves as a firm foundation for the coming age, so that they may take hold of the life that is truly life.

~ 1Timothy 6:18-19 NIV

When we grasp that this life is not all that God has in store for us, we begin to understand the next life to come. In this life, we are to use our money to do good and share generously. When we do, we build for ourselves treasure in Heaven.

Daily Inspirations From God's Word

July 27

Share with God's people who are in need. Practice hospitality. ~Romans 12:13 NIV

Many people do not invite others into their home. We don't need to have a lot to be able to share with others. Taking what we have and offering it to others with sincerity and friendship is serving as Jesus did. People who practice hospitality are greatly blessed, and bring a blessing to others.

July 28

There was an estate nearby that belonged to Publius, the chief official of the island. He welcomed us to his home and for three days entertained us hospitably. ~ Acts 28:7 NIV

After a near- death shipwreck, Paul and those on board with him were welcomed into the

Daily Inspirations From God's Word

official's home. These men were strangers and some, like Paul, were prisoners. Yet they were welcomed and treated hospitably. Being hospitable – showing care for others' needs (even strangers) – is a desirable Christian character trait.

July 29

The LORD appeared to Abraham near the great trees of Mamre while he was sitting at the entrance to his tent in the heat of the day. Abraham looked up and saw three men standing nearby. When he saw them, he hurried to the entrance of his tent to meet them and bowed low to the ground. 'Let a little water be brought, and then you may all wash your feet and rest under this tree. Let me get you something to eat, so you can be refreshed and then go on your way – now that you have come to your servant'.

~ *Genesis 18:1-2,4-5.*

Daily Inspirations From God's Word

Abraham showed hospitality with eagerness to three unexpected guests, one of which was the LORD himself. In Abraham's time, hospitality played a large role in one's reputation. Offering hospitality builds relationships among family and friends, and makes strangers feel welcome – like family.

July 30

Do not forget to show hospitality to strangers, for by so doing some people have shown hospitality to angels without knowing it.

~ Hebrews 13:2 NIV

We never know whom God may send our way. What opportunities do you have to show hospitality today? In Paul's day missionaries traveled around sharing God's Word. Many were dependent on the kindness of others, and missionaries still do this today. How much we would gain by having these dear people in our homes and by hearing stories of their missionary journeys. God might bring an angel to your table.

July 31

Offer hospitality to one another without grumbling. ~1Peter 4:9 NIV

There are many people who feel they don't have the space or the money to show hospitality. But even a small table, and a simple meal can be shared. People think of entertaining as needing to be extravagant when it really is simply making people feel welcome in your home. Hospitality is a practical way to obey God.

Daily Inspirations From God's Word

August 1

No widow may be put on the list of widows unless she is over sixty, has been faithful to her husband, and is well known for her good deeds, such as bringing up children, showing hospitality, washing the feet of saints, helping those in trouble and devoting herself to all kinds of good deeds. ~1Timothy 5:9-10 NIV

The widows list was for women of the church in need of financial support since their husbands were gone. They would work for the church in exchange for support. But there were conditions, and hospitality was among them. God still desires this act of kindness from His people.

August 2

Rather he must be hospitable, one who loves what is good, who is self-controlled, upright, holy and disciplined. ~ Titus 1:8 NIV

Daily Inspirations From God's Word

In selecting a man to be an elder in the church, we can see that it is not what they know that qualifies them, but what they do. A person's character should be examined since they will serve as a godly example to others. Among the character traits listed, is being hospitable. Is that an area that you and I need to work on? It is a desired trait.

August 3

Do not follow the crowd in doing wrong. When you give testimony in a lawsuit, do not pervert justice by siding with the crowd, and do not show favoritism to a poor person in a lawsuit.

~ Exodus 23:2-3 NIV

Often, it's money that buys people's favor. Here we are told not to favor a poor person. Rich or poor, justice should always remain impartial. Speak the truth, following the crowd leads to wrongdoing.

Daily Inspirations From God's Word

August 4
He is the Rock, his works are perfect, and all his ways are just. A faithful God who does no wrong, upright and just is he. ~ Deuteronomy 32:4 NIV

This verse is part of Moses song about God which he recited in front of all the people. It encourages us when we're reminded of God's character. He is our Rock. Unlike man, he is faithful and just and does no wrong.

August 5
For you are not a God who is pleased with wickedness; with you evil people are not welcome. The arrogant cannot stand in your presence. You hate all who do wrong.

~ Psalm 5:4-5 NIV

Those who love God want their lives to please him. We will all sin, but the follower of God

Daily Inspirations From God's Word

does not set out to commit evil against others. As we grow in faith, so does our awareness of sin in our lives. We will become more uncomfortable with and intolerant of our sin.

August 6

Naked I came from my mother's womb, and naked I will depart. The LORD gave and the LORD has taken away; may the name of the LORD be praised. In all this, Job did not sin by charging God with wrongdoing.

~ Job 1:21-22 NIV

Job had lost everything: his wife, his children, and all of his possessions. Though it was Satan's doing, God had allowed it, knowing that Job's heart was right toward him. Satan sought to disprove Job's loyalty to God by saying he only loved God for what God gave to him. But Job loved God for who he was.

Daily Inspirations From God's Word

August 7

Make sure that nobody pays back wrong for wrong, but always strive to do what is good for each other and for everyone else.

~ 1Thessalonians 5:15 NIV

It is our natural inclination to get even when someone wrongs us, to make them pay in some way. But Paul's instructions were clear: do not pay back wrong for wrong, but do good to others. This is another way the Christian stands out from those in the world. People notice when you treat someone kindly who has wronged you.

August 8

It is not rude, it is not self-seeking, it is not easily angered, it keeps no record of wrongs.

~ 1Corinthians 13:5 NIV

How do you respond to a loved one who has wronged you? Do you dishonor them by treating them rudely? Do you hold it against them and repeatedly bring the matter up? In speaking about love, Paul's list tells us to react in the opposite way. Our love should be kind and unselfish. While it may be hard not to be angry with a loved one, how we treat them after an argument shows if we are walking in the spirit or the flesh.

August 9

Hatred stirs up dissension, but love covers over all wrongs. ~ Proverbs 10:12 NIV

Do you ever hear people talking about wrong things done to them? Some people will tell anyone who will listen. Have you ever witnessed someone who gracefully changed the subject to avoid gossiping? *Love covers over all wrongs* is an eternal truth.

Daily Inspirations From God's Word

August 10

Love the Lord your God with all your heart and with all your soul and with all your mind.

~ Matthew 22:37 NIV

Jesus gave this command to the Pharisees. He also went on to say, "love your neighbor as yourself". (V 39) We can only love others if we love God first. That's why Jesus called this the first and greatest commandment.

August 11

You will keep in perfect peace him whose mind is steadfast, because he trusts in you.

~ Isaiah 26:3 NIV

Our world is full of reasons to feel troubled. Chaos can be all around us, but when we concentrate our thoughts on God's Word and trust in Him, He keep our minds at peace.

August 12

I the LORD search the heart and examine the mind, to reward a man according to his conduct, according to what his deeds deserve.

~Jeremiah 17:10 NIV

What will God find when he searches our hearts and minds? Are we following his ways and trusting in him? Or, are we following man's ways and trusting in ourselves? What sinful thoughts are in our hearts and minds? Are we taking sinful thoughts captive to the obedience of Christ? (2 Corinthians 10:5) Our conduct will reveal what is in our hearts.

August 13

Do not conform any longer to the pattern of this world, but be transformed by the renewing of your mind. Then you will be able to test and

Daily Inspirations From God's Word

approve what God's will is – his good, pleasing and perfect will. ~ Romans 12:2 NIV

The Lord instructs us to change the pattern of our thinking. A wise person once said, "what goes into the mind, comes out in a life". We renew our minds with God's Word. When we read it, it transforms our thinking, helps us to discern God's will; and we learn to live according to His ways.

August 14

The mind of sinful man is death, but the mind controlled by the Spirit is life and peace; the sinful mind is hostile to God.

~ Romans 8:6-7 NIV

Either the sinful nature or the Holy Spirit within us controls us. Those who have chosen Jesus have chosen life, but can still yield to the

Doreen Wennberg   155

sinful nature. We must consciously choose to follow the Holy Spirit daily, which will bring peace into our lives.

August 15

Then he opened their minds so they could understand the scriptures. ~ Luke 24:45 NIV

After Jesus rose from the dead, he appeared to the disciples. They still did not understand much of what he had told them during his 3 years with them. So he opened their minds to understand the Scriptures. He does the same for us today. When we ask him to help us understand, He gives us insight as we read and study His Word. Are you asking for understanding?

August 16

The god of this age has blinded the minds of unbelievers, so that they cannot see the light of the gospel of the glory of Christ, who is the image of God. ~2 Corinthians 4:4 NIV

Though the gospel is available to everyone, not everyone will choose to believe. Satan, the god of this age, deceives people by making sinful things seem appealing. This is one of his ways of blinding unbelievers to the light of the gospel.

August 17

David said to the Philistine, 'You come against me with the sword and spear and javelin, but I come against you in the name of the LORD Almighty, the God of the armies of Israel, whom you have defied. All those gathered here will know that it is not by sword or spear that the

Daily Inspirations From God's Word

LORD saves; for the battle is the LORD's, and he will give all of you into our hands.

~ 1Samuel 17:45,47 NIV

David was just a young shepherd boy when he said this to Goliath. David had great trust in the LORD, because he had experienced God's care when he shepherded his flock from the attacks of wild bears and lions. (See 1Sam. 17:34-37). David knew the living God, and he was confident that in this battle, God would deliver Goliath into his hand. How well do you know the living Lord? And how much do you trust him to fight your battles?

August 18

He said: 'Listen, King Jehoshaphat and all who live in Judah and Jerusalem! This is what the LORD says to you: 'Do not be afraid or

discouraged because of this vast army. For the
battle is not yours, but God's.

~ *2Chronicles 20:15 NIV*

King Jehoshaphat had been informed that a great army was advancing toward him. His first reaction was to pray. He called all of Judah to fast, and the people assembled in the Lord's temple. (2Chronicles 20:3-12). God heard the cries of the people and spoke through one young man, Jahaziel. (2Chronicles 20:14). He reminded them not to be afraid, because the battle was not theirs, but the Lord's. The enemy armies that come against us come in many forms. Similar to Jehoshaphat, our first response to great calamity should be to call upon the Lord. When we take the stance that those battles are not ours, but God's, we call upon His name for help, and watch as He fights our battles.

August 19

Who is this King of glory? The LORD strong and mighty, the LORD mighty in battle.

~ Psalm 24:8 NIV

The Psalms are expressions of poetry written to praise God and worship him. Psalms are songs. This one was often set to music, proclaiming who God is. When we praise God, we recognize and appreciate how great and mighty He is. What is your perspective of God? Do you see Him as 'strong and mighty, the LORD mighty in battle?'

August 20

I have seen something else under the sun: The race is not to the swift or the battle to the strong, nor does food come to the wise or wealth to the brilliant or favor to the learned; but time and chance happen to them all.

~ Ecclesiastes 9:11 NIV

Daily Inspirations From God's Word

Solomon describes an unfair set of circumstances that we also experience in our present world, where evil seems to prevail. Sin sometimes appears to win the battle. Even so, we must continue to trust and serve God, because we know Who has really won the war.

August 21

This is what the LORD said to me: 'As a lion growls, a great lion over his prey – and though a whole band of shepherds is called together against him, he is not frightened by their shouts or disturbed by their clamor – so the LORD Almighty will come down to do battle on Mount Zion and on its heights. ~ Isaiah 31:4 NIV

God is not a mortal that he fears anyone or anything. He is like a mighty lion. Though many evil armies come against his people, the

Daily Inspirations From God's Word

LORD Almighty will come down to do battle. We must not forget how powerful God is.

August 22

In everything he did he had great success, because the LORD was with him. David and his men went out and killed two hundred Philistines. The Philistine commanders continued to go out to battle, and as often as they did, David met with more success than the rest of Saul's officers, and his name became well known.

~ 1Samuel 18:14 NIV

Because the LORD was with David, he killed many Philistines, Goliath was his first. The Philistines, powerful enemies, continued to come against Israel, but David overcame them.

We have a persistent enemy who continually comes against us. But God is with us, and like

He did for David, God is able to give us success over our enemies.

August 23

With him is only the arm of flesh, but with us is the LORD our God to help us and to fight our battles. ~2 Chronicles 32:8 NIV

Although the king of Assyria was a powerful enemy of Judah, Hezekiah knew the greater power who was with him – the Lord God Almighty. King Hezekiah trusted in God. He knew that God would help the people fight their battles. How confident are you that God is with you to help you to fight your battles? The more time you spend with God, the more you will be confident and trust His power to fight for you.

August 24

Now faith is being sure of what we hope for and certain of what we do not see.

~ Hebrews 11:1 NIV

When we hope for something we usually have waited some time for it. When we don't see what we're waiting and hoping for, we can become discouraged. But faith is confident in God. We trust in God's promises even when we don't see them happening because, we know that he is faithful.

August 25

By faith, we understand that the universe was formed at God's command, so that what is seen was not made out of what was visible.

~ Hebrews 11:3 NIV

Daily Inspirations From God's Word

No one was there when God formed the universe from nothing. He spoke and it came to be. Our understanding of that miracle can only be by faith in the power of God's Word, which is mighty.

August 26

Some men brought to him a paralyzed man, lying on a mat. When Jesus saw their faith, he said to the man, 'Take heart, son; your sins are forgiven.'
~ Matthew 9:2 NIV

Jesus saw the faith of the man's friends. They believed if they just got their friend to Jesus, His power would heal him. Jesus healed him by saying, "Your sins are forgiven". He knew that the man wasn't only paralyzed physically but spiritually. More than anything else, we need forgiveness from Jesus.

August 27

And he did not do many miracles there because of their lack of faith. ~ Matthew 13:58 NIV

In Jesus' own hometown of Nazareth, the people did not believe in Jesus. Perhaps the familiarity with him, blinded them to who he really was. Lack of faith can keep us from experiencing God's power in our life. We can ask God to increase our faith and help us overcome our unbelief, and then expect to see Him act.

August 28

We live by faith not by sight.

~ 2 Corinthians 5:7 NIV

What does it mean to have faith? Faith is believing in what we can't see. Our preference is to believe because we see, like the disciple Thomas. (See John 20:24-29), but that is not faith. To live by faith and not sight means we praise God and expect change, even when our circumstances don't look different.

August 29

In him and through faith in him we may approach God with freedom and confidence.

~ Ephesians 3:12 NIV

Before Christ's death, there was a barrier – our sin – that kept us from approaching God. At Christ's death, the curtain in the temple tore in two, symbolizing that the barrier between God and man was removed. Because Christ paid the sacrifice for our sins, all people are free to approach God through faith in his son.

Daily Inspirations From God's Word

August 30

We do not want you to become lazy, but to imitate those who through faith and patience inherit what has been promised. And so after waiting patiently, Abraham received what was promised. ~ Hebrews 6:12,15 NIV

It's so easy to grow weary and become lazy in the faith when the wait for what we hope for seems particularly long. Abraham waited twenty-five years for the son God promised. He is an example of a faithful man who waits for God's timing. When your wait seems long, remember Abraham and imitate his faith.

August 31

If my people, who are called by my name, will humble themselves and pray and seek my face and turn from their wicked ways, then will I hear

Daily Inspirations From God's Word

from heaven and will forgive their sin and will heal their land. ~ 2Chronicles 7:14 NIV

God looks for repentant hearts that are willing to turn from wickedness. When we humbly admit our sin, and pray for forgiveness, we can expect God to answer our prayers.

September 1

Listen to my cry for help, my King and my God, for to you I pray. In the morning, LORD, you hear my voice; in the morning I lay my requests before you and wait expectantly.

~ Psalm 5:2-3 NIV

Our prayers are communication with God. They don't have to be fancy or long, but they show our dependence on God. Some people choose to talk to him before getting out of bed, others talk over coffee, and some on their

Daily Inspirations From God's Word

morning commute. Whatever you choose, include God in your morning, bring your requests to him and watch him direct your path that day.

September 2

When I heard these things, I sat down and wept. For some days I mourned and fasted and prayed before the God of heaven.

~ Nehemiah 1:4 NIV

Have you ever received news that made you break down and cry? In Nehemiah's day, the walls of Jerusalem had not been rebuilt. The people were in sin and left the walls broken down, leaving them defenseless and open to attack. Nehemiah was distraught and sought the Lord. When news devastates us, like Nehemiah, our sorrow should lead us to pray.

September 3

They were helped in fighting them, and God handed the Hagrites and all their allies over to them, because they cried out to him during the battle. He answered their prayers, because they trusted in him. ~ 1Chronicles 5:20 NIV

This scripture refers to the armies of Reuben, Gad, and Manasseh. God helped them in their battle against the enemy, because even though they were trained to fight, they didn't trust in themselves. They trusted in God. Our training is in vain unless we look to the Lord for help to fight our battles.

September 4

The Spirit helps us in our weakness. We do not know what we ought to pray for, but the Spirit himself intercedes for us with groans that words cannot express. ~ Romans 8:26 NIV

Daily Inspirations From God's Word

Have you ever had a time in prayer where you don't have a word to express your heart? Perhaps your heart is troubled and the pain is too deep for words. It's during those times that the Spirit intercedes for us when we can't find words. He hears our heart without even an utterance from us.

September 5

And pray in the Spirit on all occasions with all kinds of prayers and requests. With this in mind, be alert and always keep praying for all the Lord's people. ~ Ephesians 6:18 NIV

We are told to be alert so that we can intercede for others. We can pray on all occasions by praying short "arrow" prayers throughout the day. We form a habit of praying in our mind, under our breath, and in response to all things. Prayer becomes a part of everything – even the world news. Are you alert to the headlines so that you can pray for other people?

September 6

The prayer of a righteous man is powerful and effective. ~ James 5:16b NIV

The most powerful thing the Believer can do is pray. To be righteous means to be right with God. So the person who has confessed their sins is right with God and has no barrier, which makes their prayers powerful and effective!

September 7

Wealth and honor come from you; you are the ruler of all things. But who am I, and who are my people, that we should give as generously as this?

Daily Inspirations From God's Word

Everything comes from you, and we have given you only what comes from your hand.
~ 1Chronicles 12,14 NIV

David knew and understood that everything they had came from God's hand. When people think that because they've worked hard for their money, it belongs to them, they're mistaken.

By acknowledging that all our accomplishments, talents and abilities come from God, we gain the right perspective.

September 8
O LORD, God of Israel, there is no God like you in heaven or on earth — you who keep your covenant of love with your servants who continue wholeheartedly in your way. You have kept your promise to your servant David my father; with

your mouth you have promised and with your hand you have fulfilled it – as it is today.

~ 2 Chronicles 6:14-15 NIV

In front of the people, Solomon acknowledged that God was true to his Word. God is faithful; his hand will always fulfill the promises his mouth has spoken.

September 9

For day and night your hand was heavy upon me; my strength was sapped as in the heat of summer. Then I acknowledged my sin to you and did not cover up my iniquity. I said, 'I will confess my transgressions to the LORD' – and you forgave the guilt of my sin. ~ Psalm 32:4-5 NIV

If you ever lied as a child, or broke something valuable and tried to cover it up, you might remember the feeling of guilt when your mother questioned you. Usually a parent knows when their child has done wrong. They're just waiting for a confession. If you love the LORD and choose not to acknowledge your sin, similar to earthly parents, you'll experience the heaviness of his hand. Though he already knows it. He's just waiting for you to confess it to him, and is ready to forgive when you do.

September 10

If the LORD delights in a man's way, he makes his steps firm; though he stumble, he will not fall, for the LORD upholds him with his hand.

~ Psalm 37: 23-24 NIV

Children learning to walk are also learning to follow and trust. God loves for us to follow him and trust him. As children learning to walk may stumble, – we can too. But God's hand is there to steady us and make our steps firm.

September 11

Yet, O LORD, you are our Father. We are the clay, you are the potter; we are all the work of your hand. ~ Isaiah 64:8 NIV

As the potter forms the clay into his creation, so God forms us by his hand into creative works of art. The potter's wheel spins a long time as he works, molding and shaping the clay until it's formed into a beautiful image. Each of us is a work in progress. It takes time as the Master molds and forms us into the exact image he is creating us to be.

Daily Inspirations From God's Word

September 12
Dogs have surrounded me; a band of evil men has encircled me, they have pierced my hands and feet. ~ Psalm 22: 16 NIV

In crying out to God about his own troubles, David was prophesying about the Lord Jesus, hundreds of years before his crucifixion happened. May we never forget the great suffering that Jesus willingly endured at the hands of evil men, ensured our freedom for all eternity.

September 13
My sheep listen to my voice; I know them, and they follow me. I give them eternal life, and they shall never perish; no one can snatch them out of my hand. ~ John 10:27-28 NIV

Because sheep are familiar with the shepherd's voice, they follow him. The shepherd protects them and refuses to let anyone take them from him. If we know the Lord, we will know his voice and listen to him. We are safe. He will not let anything or anyone take us from his hand.

September 14

Walk in all the way that the LORD your God has commanded you, so that you may live and prosper and prolong your days in the land that you will possess. ~ Deuteronomy 5:33 NIV

In the Old Testament, God gave the Ten Commandments to Moses for the people to follow. They are standards for right living. The law was the Old Testament covenant. In the New Testament, we have entered into covenant with God through his Son Jesus. God requires people then and now to walk in his ways, so that we may live right and be prosperous.

September 15

Blessed is the man who does not walk in the counsel of the wicked or stand in the seat of mockers. But his delight is in the law of the LORD, and on his law he meditates day and night. ~ Psalm 1:1-2 NIV

The people we associate with can be either bad or good influences in our lives and affect our walk with God. If we have friends who are indifferent to the Word of God, their attitude can rub off on us if we're not careful. If we have friends who agree with our belief in God, they will build up and encourage our faith. When we spend time meditating - reading and thinking about God's Word, we will learn to live as God wants us to and be blessed by him.

Daily Inspirations From God's Word

September 16

Even though I walk through the valley of the shadow of death, I will fear no evil, for you are with me; your rod and staff, they comfort me.

~ Psalm 23:4 NIV

We will all walk through the shadow of death at some point. When we know God, we will have no fear. We know he is with us and his presence greatly comforts us.

September 17

Listen, my son, accept what I say, and the years of your life will be many. When you walk, your steps will not be hampered; when you run, you will not stumble. ~ Proverbs 4:10,12 NIV

God speaks to all his sons and daughters to listen and accept his words. Some children refuse and will bear the consequences of many falls. Some children will choose to obey and will walk and run without stumbling.

September 18
Whether you turn to the right or to the left, your ears will hear a voice behind you, saying, 'This is the way; walk in it.' ~ Isaiah 30:21NIV

We can easily get lost on life's path and need correction. When we study God's Word, we become familiar with the Spirit's voice leading us. We know when he says, "turn this way or that" and we will know which way to walk.

September 19
If we claim to have fellowship with him yet walk

in the darkness, we lie and do not live by the truth. But if we walk in the light, we have fellowship with one another, and the blood of Jesus, his Son, purifies us from all sin.

~ 1 John 1:6-7 NIV

We cannot continue to live in darkness if we claim to have a relationship with God. That is lying. Once you turn a light on, darkness is dispelled. This is how a believer's life will look. What was once dark in their life will flee, because they walk in the light. Their darkness (sin) was turned to light by the purifying blood of Jesus. The believer will still sin and need forgiveness, but they will not willfully, rebelliously live and walk in darkness.

September 20

And this is love: that we walk in obedience to his commands. As you have heard from the beginning, his command is that you walk in love. ~ 2 John 1:6 NIV

Loving as God commands means loving one another when it is difficult. It means choosing to serve those who may not deserve it. We can also show love by not judging and by accepting people. We walk in love because God commands it.

September 21

He is like a tree planted by streams of water, which yields its fruit in season and whose leaf does not wither. Whatever he does prospers.

~ Psalm 1:3 NIV

The first two verses of this Psalm talk about those who do not walk with the wicked, but delight in and meditate on God's Word. (Psalm 1:1-2). The picture here in verse three is of a thriving tree, whose roots are fed by the

Daily Inspirations From God's Word

stream. When we are full of God's Word we thrive and bear fruit; our lives are vibrant and full of abundance. God prospers – gives favor or success – to those who apply His Word.

September 22

The fruit of the righteous is a tree of life, and he who wins souls is wise. ~ Proverbs 11:30 NIV

The spiritual fruit we bear when walking with God changes lives. As we share His truth with those who don't know Him, they are brought from death to life.

September 23

The fruit of righteousness will be peace.
~ Isaiah 32:17a NIV

Daily Inspirations From God's Word

The righteous person can have peace within despite conflicts and turmoil that surrounds him or her.

September 24

He will be like a tree planted by the water that sends out its roots by the stream. It does not fear when heat comes; its leaves are always green. It has no worries in a year of drought and never fails to bear fruit. ~ Jeremiah 17:8 NIV

In the Bible, trees are often depicted as symbols of fruitful lives. A mighty tree is a picture of great strength, not because of itself, but because its roots have grown deep. A tree planted by the water has a continual source. God is our source. When we stay rooted in God, we will not fear when the heat of life comes, when the economy fails, or when disaster strikes. Our lives will never fail to bear fruit when we trust in God.

Daily Inspirations From God's Word

September 25

I am the true vine, and my Father is the gardener. He cuts off every branch in me that bears no fruit, while every branch that does bear fruit he prunes so that it will be even more fruitful.

~ John 15:1-2 NIV

A gardener knows that cutting back a branch will promote more growth in flowers or fruit. Sometimes the gardener cuts branches off when they produce nothing. They are worthless and can even infect the rest of the plant. Here Jesus explains that he is the vine and his true followers are the fruitful branches. God the Father separates unfruitful branches, cutting them off from the source while he prunes the fruitful ones for more growth. Which describes you? Is your commitment to God superficial, in danger of being cut off? Or does your commitment to God show evidence of a Christ-like life, ready for more growth?

Daily Inspirations From God's Word

September 26

And we pray this in order that you may live a life worthy of the Lord and may please him in every way: bearing fruit in every good work, growing in knowledge of God. ~ Colossians 1:10 NIV

Knowledge of God's will, spiritual wisdom and understanding are the things Paul prayed for the Colossians. (See v 9). Like Paul, when we pray the same for others, we desire that their lives please and honor God and bear good fruit. Someone who is growing in the knowledge of God will produce good fruit. Do you pray this for others and yourself?

September 27

But the fruit of the spirit is love, joy, peace, patience, kindness, goodness, faithfulness, gentleness and self-control.

~ Galatians 5:22 NIV

Daily Inspirations From God's Word

These are the character traits that the Spirit produces and grows in the believer's life. Every one of these fruits has an opposite that reflects the sinful nature. A believer reflects Christ's nature having joined their life with his. The level of the life of these qualities will be evident by the more you know, love and study God's Word.

September 28

The LORD turn his face toward you and give you peace. ~ Numbers 6:26 NIV

There are five parts of this priestly blessing spoken over the Israelite people. This was the last part of it.

Asking the Lord to turn his face toward someone is to ask for his approval for them. We encourage others when we pray for them with these words of blessing.

Daily Inspirations From God's Word

September 29

Turn from evil and do good; seek peace and pursue it. ~ Psalm 34:14 NIV

When a person chooses to follow God, they choose to turn away from morally wrong behavior. A person who loves the Lord seeks to do good to others and works at having peace. If we live and respond by actively seeking peace and finding it, we will find harmony in all our relationships.

September 30

Pray for the peace of Jerusalem: May those who love you be secure. ~ Psalm 122:6 NIV

Although David wrote this psalm hundreds of years before Christ was rejected, he was interceding prophetically on behalf of the people of Jerusalem to be at peace with God.

Daily Inspirations From God's Word

Jerusalem believed in God the Father but rejected his Son. Because of that rejection, Jerusalem is not at peace with God. They are not eternally secure. May we join them in this prayer.

October 1

When a man's ways are pleasing to the LORD, he makes even his enemies to be at peace with him. ~ Proverbs 16:7 NIV

Living a life pleasing to the Lord results in healing and restoration, even between enemies.

October 2

You will keep in perfect peace him whose mind is steadfast, because he trusts in you.

~ Isaiah 26:3 NIV

Daily Inspirations From God's Word

In the midst of chaos, God's Word reminds us that when we keep our mind fixed on him and not the problem, trusting him, we receive inner peace.

October 3

For to us a child is born, to us a son is given, and the government will be on his shoulders. And he will be called Wonderful Counselor, Mighty God, Everlasting Father, Prince of Peace.

~ Isaiah 9:6 NIV

Isaiah foretells the birth of Christ during a time of great darkness, offering the people hope. Four hundred years later God fulfills this prophecy. Isaiah uses four royal names to describe Jesus the Messiah. Wonderful Counselor: The One who will advise us. Mighty God: God himself; Everlasting Father: Without beginning or end, our father. Prince of Peace: His government brings peace.

Daily Inspirations From God's Word

October 4

No discipline seems pleasing at the time, but painful. Later on, however, it produces a harvest of righteousness and peace for those who have been trained by it. ~ Hebrews 12:11 NIV

There are some parents who allow their children to run wild, with no boundaries or rules. But parents who discipline their children, do so because they love them and are training them to learn right from wrong. Discipline is not easy but it's necessary. Just as a parent disciplines, God the Father does. It is from his heart of love for us, and for our good. Discipline from God produces righteousness and peace in our lives.

October 5

In the beginning God created the heavens and the earth. Now the earth was formless and

Daily Inspirations From God's Word

empty, darkness was over the surface of the deep, and the Spirit of God was hovering over the waters. And God said, 'let there be light,' and there was light. ~ Genesis 1:1-3 NIV

Don't you find it amazing that God the Creator spoke, and on the first day the darkness became light.

October 6

By day the LORD went ahead of them in a pillar of cloud to guide them on their way and by night in a pillar of fire to give them light, so that they could travel by day or night.

~ Exodus 13:21 NIV

The LORD God appeared to the Israelites in different forms to guide, protect and give them light. Jesus, the light of the world, is always with us, to guide, protect and light our way.

October 7

You are my lamp, O LORD; the LORD turns my darkness into light. ~ 2 Samuel 22:29 NIV

If you've ever walked through a discouraging dark time in your life, then you know the deep pain and sorrow that it can bring. Serious illness, the loss of a loved one, or divorce can cause us to feel hopeless. During our times of deepest darkness, God's light shines the brightest. God always makes a way for his light to shine through. So you can say like David, 'You are my Lamp, O LORD', and thank him for it!

Daily Inspirations From God's Word

October 8

Your word is a lamp to my feet and a light for my path. ~ Psalm 119:105 NIV

No one hikes a mountain at night. They know they wouldn't be able to see their way. They might stumble and fall. We live in a dark, corrupt world. In order to navigate it safely, we need God's Word to light the way. When you study the Bible, it lights your path and shows you the correct way to go.

October 9

The light shines in the darkness, but the darkness has not understood it. ~ John 1:5 NIV

Men who did not understand the light, crucified the Messiah. Similarly, people today who don't understand the light reject Jesus.

Daily Inspirations From God's Word

The light shines in the darkness to help us see ourselves as people in need of a Savior.

October 10

God is light; in him there is no darkness at all.
~ 1John 1:5 NIV

God is holy and pure. There is no imperfection in him. Light represents God's purity and holiness. Darkness represents evil. God's light always exposes the sin of darkness.

October 11

The city does not need the sun or the moon to shine on it, for the glory of God gives it light, and the Lamb is its lamp. ~ Revelation 21:23 NIV

Daily Inspirations From God's Word

This new city will be different from any other city we've ever seen. It will not need anything but the glory of God to give it light. The light of God that represents all that is holy and pure will radiate throughout the city. What a glorious sight that will be!

October 12

For all have sinned and fall short of the glory of God, and are justified freely by his grace through the redemption that came by Christ Jesus.

~ Romans 3:23-24 NIV

All of us have done wrong. All crime has consequences. Some crimes receive greater penalties than others, but all crimes are punishable. Similarly, all sin – no matter its size – is punishable. Being justified freely means being declared not guilty. Because of

Christ's death, we are pardoned and redeemed by his grace.

October 13

But he said to me, my grace is sufficient for you, for my power is made perfect in weakness.

~ 2 Corinthians 12:9 NIV

The world's way is the opposite of the Lord's way. The worlds way is to take credit for what you accomplish in your own strength. God's way helps us to realize our weakness. Then when we accomplish something, everyone knows that his grace is at work in us. This shows his power, and the glory goes to him, not us.

October 14

But because of his great love for us, God, who is

rich in mercy, made us alive in Christ even when we were dead in transgressions – it is by grace you have been saved. ~ Ephesians 2:4-5 NIV

As sinners we are spiritually dead. But God's love and mercy gives life to sinful people. Not because of any work we've done; not because of church or Christian family status; but because of God's grace that we have been saved.

October 15

Let us then approach the throne of grace with confidence, so that we may receive mercy and find grace to help us in our time of need.

~ Hebrews 4:16 NIV

Before Jesus' death, the people could not approach God alone. The high priest was the only one allowed into the Most Holy Place to make atonement for the people's sins. Now,

Daily Inspirations From God's Word

Jesus is the great high priest who ascended into heaven and made atonement for our sins with his own blood. Knowing this gives us boldness in prayer to approach the throne of grace ourselves. We come with confidence knowing that God's mercy is there to help us with our needs.

October 16

See to it that no one misses the grace of God and that no bitter root grows up to cause trouble and defile many. ~ Hebrews 12:15 NIV

We can allow hurts to fester and grow. Like a weed that destroys a garden, a bitter root can destroy relationships. God gives us grace to deal with hurts caused by others. But when we insist on holding grudges, we miss the grace he gives us and risk ruining the relationship. We show God's power at work in our lives when we show grace to others.

Daily Inspirations From God's Word

October 17

God opposes the proud, but gives grace to the humble. ~ James 4:6 NIV

God hates pride. When we humble ourselves before God and others, he gives us grace.

October 18

But grow in the grace and knowledge of our Lord and Savior Jesus Christ. ~ 2 Peter 3:18 NIV

When we spend time with loved ones, we get to know them better. This is also true of spending time with the Lord. It is important to continue to study God's Word, so that we can grow in his grace and knowledge. This is the best way to get to know him better and better.

Daily Inspirations From God's Word

October 19

So Lot chose for himself the whole plain of the Jordan and set out toward the east.

~ Genesis 13:11 NIV

Lot's Uncle Abraham gave him first choice of a place to live in the land. Instead of giving his elder the best share of the land, he chose the best for himself and his family. Lot's choice showed greed. What do our choices show about us? How do our choices show consideration for others?

October 20

Blessed is the nation whose God is the LORD, the people he chose for his inheritance.

~ Psalm 33:12 NIV

God chose the nation of Israel and demonstrated his love to the world through

Daily Inspirations From God's Word

them. We gentile nations are included in the blessing and inheritance when we make God our LORD.

October 21

If you belonged to the world, it would love you as its own. As it is, you do not belong to the world, but I have chosen you out of the world. That is why the world hates you. ~ John 15:19 NIV

Every battle has two sides. Those in the world are on one side; those who belong to Christ are on the other. The world would love us if we were on their side. If you believe in God it is because he chose you out of the world. That is why the world hates Christians.

October 22

But God chose the foolish things of the world to shame the wise; God chose the weak things of the world to shame the strong.

~ 1 Corinthians 1:27 NIV

There are many intellectually gifted people in the world. Yet God chooses to use those who would be considered less than others. God chooses to work through the weak things rather than the strong, because it shows his power.

October 23

For he chose us in him before the creation of the world to be holy and blameless in his sight.

~ Ephesians 1:4 NIV

God had a plan long before we were born, before the creation of this world. He chose us in him to be holy and blameless. Though he knew we would be sinful, he had a plan through Christ to save us.

October 24

But you are a chosen people, royal priesthood, a holy nation, a people belonging to God, that you may declare the praises of him who called you out of darkness into his wonderful light.

~ 1 Peter 2:9 NIV

Christ's death and victory on the cross gave man access to God. There is no more need for the priest to go before God on our behalf. Jesus did that. Now we, as priests, can join in his work. We bring others to be reconciled to God by sharing what he has done.

Daily Inspirations From God's Word

October 25

But only one thing is needed. Mary has chosen what is better, and it will not be taken away from her. ~ Luke 10:42 NIV

In this passage, Mary chose to sit and listen to the Lord who was visiting in her home. Her sister Martha complained that she was left to do all of the work. When we, like Mary, choose to learn more about Jesus, it is always the best choice.

October 26

Do not seek revenge or bear a grudge against one of your people, but love your neighbor as yourself.
~ Leviticus 19:18 NIV

Getting revenge and holding grudges are not God's way. His way is to forgive, and to love others.

Daily Inspirations From God's Word

October 27

*But if from there you seek the LORD your God,
you will find him if you look for him with all your
heart and with all your soul.*

~ Deuteronomy 4:29 NIV

We find the LORD when we pray. We find
him when we search for his presence, and
when we sit quietly before him. When we
think about God and meditate on his Word,
we find he is there, within the stillness of our
heart.

October 28

*For the Son of Man came to seek and save what
was lost. ~ Luke 19:10 NIV*

Jesus didn't go to those who were considered
righteous, who knew and kept the law. He
didn't avoid despised outcasts or immoral
people. Jesus loved them and sought them. In

Daily Inspirations From God's Word

what way can we follow Jesus' example to seek out those who are lost, so that they too may be saved?

October 29
But those who seek the LORD lack no good thing.
~ Psalm 34:10b NIV

Some people seek the Lord and expect to get everything they ask for. Seeking God doesn't guarantee that we receive all we want. We lack nothing when we have the LORD. He is all we need.

October 30
But seek first his kingdom and his righteousness, and all these things will be given to you as well.
~ Matthew 6:33 NIV

Daily Inspirations From God's Word

What things worry you? Some people stress over everything in their life. Rather than worry about all the details, Jesus tells us to seek him first. What priority does Jesus have over everything else in your life? He knows our needs and will supply them. Don't let the worries of life rob you of what is most important – time with Jesus.

October 31

Look to the LORD and his strength; seek his face always. ~ Psalm 105:4 NIV

It is easy to get off track. Distractions are all around us. We can slip from looking to God, and look to ourselves or others for help. Our help comes from no one but the Lord. What are you doing to ensure that you are looking to his strength alone. What will you do to prevent distractions from keeping you from seeking God?

November 1

And without faith it is impossible to please God, because anyone who comes to him must believe that he exists and that he rewards those who earnestly seek him. ~ Hebrews 11:6 NIV

Nothing we do pleases God more than faith. We can't come to know him by the work we do. We come to know him through our belief in his existence and in his Son, Jesus Christ. Faith is believing in what we cannot see, but we know it's real. We need not understand everything to have faith. How is your faith in God helping you to see that he rewards those who earnestly seek him?

November 2

The LORD will fulfill his purpose for me; your love, O LORD, endures forever – do not abandon the works of your hands. ~ Psalm 138:8 NIV

David made a statement of faith. He believed that God would fulfill His purpose for David's life. We need to believe that too, and boldly state it.

November 3

It is better not to vow than to make a vow and not fulfill it. ~ Ecclesiastes 5:5

People make promises and break them all the time. Those who are the victims of broken promises are hurt and disappointed by them. That's why Solomon instructs us not to make a vow. If we do make vows, we should exhibit the integrity to fulfill them.

Daily Inspirations From God's Word

November 4

From the east I summon a bird of prey; from a far-off land, a man to fulfill my purpose. What I have said, that will I bring about; what I have planned, that will I do. ~ Isaiah 46:11

This comes from the passage which speaks about the gods of Babylon. Isaiah refers to the bird from a far off land and speaks of a wicked man named Cyrus. God used him to carry out his judgment on Babylon. God will use whomever he chooses to accomplish his purpose.

November 5

Hope deferred makes the heart sick, but a longing fulfilled is a tree of life.

~ Proverbs 13:12 NIV

When hope is withheld or delayed it can cause

great heartache. But when our hope changes to a reality, it becomes a great blessing.

November 6

Now I am about to go the way of all the earth. You know with all your heart and soul that not one of all the good promises the LORD your God gave you has failed. Every promise has been fulfilled; not one has failed. But just as all the good things the LORD your God has promised you have come to you, so he will bring on you all the evil things he has threatened, until the LORD your God has destroyed you from this good land he has given you. ~ Joshua 23:14 NIV

As Joshua was dying, he reminded the people that God was faithful and fulfilled every promise he had made. However, Joshua knew that if the people disobeyed God, their actions would bring about consequences that God would punish. The same is true for us. As God's children, He rewards and corrects us according to our behavior.

November 7
He fulfills the desires of those who fear him.
~ Psalm 145:19 NIV

Those who have a reverential awe of God can expect Him to fulfill their desires.

November 8
I am not referring to all of you; I know those I have chosen. But this is to fulfill the scripture: 'He who shares my bread has lifted up his heel against me.' I am telling you now before it

Daily Inspirations From God's Word

happens, so that when it does happen you will
believe that I am He. ~ John 13:18-19 NIV

There were numerous prophecies fulfilled
during Jesus' life, death and resurrection. We
know that this prediction referred to Judas,
once a close friend, (Psalm 41:9) who would
later betray Jesus. God's Word can be trusted
because it is true. The fulfillment of the Old
Testament scriptures testify to this fact.

November 9
To fear the LORD is to hate evil; I hate pride and
arrogance, evil behavior and perverse speech.
                              ~ Proverbs 8:13 NIV

Those who love the LORD love what he loves,
and hate what he hates. Cultivate desirable
behavior in yourself that displays a kind,

Daily Inspirations From God's Word

humble nature and speaks sweetly to others. This pleases the LORD.

November 10
Pride only breeds quarrels, but wisdom is found in those who take advice. ~ Proverbs 13:10 NIV

Those who are full of themselves think they know it all, and they cause trouble. A humble person is teachable.

November 11
Live in harmony with one another. Do not be proud, but be willing to associate with people of low position. Do not be conceited.

~ Romans 12:16 NIV

Some people think more highly of themselves

because of their status, and they look down on those they consider beneath them. But God doesn't see status. God looks at a person's heart. Strive to treat all people the same, no matter what their standing is.

November 12
Pride goes before destruction, a haughty spirit before a fall. ~ Proverbs 16:18 NIV

Pride corrupts our thinking. One can achieve great amounts of wealth, success, education, or fame, and think so highly of themselves that their attitude of "I'm better, smarter and more important than you," will eventually bring them down. Be a wise person who always gives God the glory for any achievement.

Daily Inspirations From God's Word

November 13

Your heart became proud on account of your beauty, and you corrupted your wisdom because of your splendor. So I threw you to earth; I made a spectacle of you before kings.

~ Ezekiel 28:17NIV

We know that God created Satan as a beautiful angel. But because he became proud and tried to usurp God's authority, God threw him out of heaven. A person can be exalted to a high position and forget who gave him his success. Don't let your heart become proud as you progress up the ladder.

November 14

And those who walk in pride he is able to humble.

~ Daniel 4:37b NIV

This was spoken by King Nebuchadnezzar,

Daily Inspirations From God's Word

because he had experienced God's judgment when he became too proud of his kingdom. (Daniel 4:1-36). God warned him in a dream to repent of his pride, but he did not. When Nebuchadnezzar finally raised his eyes toward heaven and acknowledged the LORD, God restored him. When God's Word warns us to repent of our pride, we'd better humble ourselves or God will.

November 15

God opposes the proud but gives grace to the humble. ~ James 4:6b NIV

Why does God oppose the proud? Pride shows a "me attitude", a self-centered attitude. God is giving and humble, and expects his followers to be.

Daily Inspirations From God's Word

November 16

A gentle answer turns away wrath, but a harsh word stirs up wrath. ~ Proverbs 15:1 NIV

We always have a choice of what comes out of our mouths. We can choose to start something or end something. Be humble; choose the latter.

November 17

Take my yoke upon you and learn from me, for I am gentle and humble in heart, and you will find rest for your souls. ~ Matthew 11:29 NIV

A wooden yoke is made for two, not one. Oxen must work together. One cannot go one way while the other goes a different way. They must walk together, and so must we with Christ. We can do nothing of eternal value apart from Him. Working apart from Jesus will wear us out. To take his yoke upon us is to learn from him and receive rest. He is not forceful, but gentle. He knows the way, and he's humble.

November 18

The LORD said, 'Go out and stand on the mountain in the presence of the LORD, for the LORD is about to pass by.' Then a great and powerful wind tore the mountains apart and shattered the rocks before the LORD, but the LORD was not in the wind. After the wind there was an earthquake. But the LORD was not in the earthquake. After the earthquake came a fire, but the LORD was not in the fire. And after the fire came a gentle whisper. ~ 1Kings 19:12NIV

God is powerful and his power creates and controls all things. But he doesn't only reveal himself to us in great and mighty acts. More often it is in the still small voice of his gentle whisper.

Daily Inspirations From God's Word

November 19

Be completely humble and gentle; be patient, bearing with one another in love.

~ Ephesians 4:2 NIV

People often display less patience when they're among family and friends. Perhaps it's because they take those they love for granted. Family members need and deserve humble, gentle, and patient attitudes from loved ones. Ask God what you can do to help your family dynamics run smooth.

November 20

Let your gentleness be evident to all.

~ Philippians 4:5 NIV

Some people are not naturally gentle. Some people are more abrupt and harsh in their manner of speaking. If that's you, ask God to help you be gentler, so that others see him through you.

November 21

Your beauty should not come from outward adornment, such as braided hair and the wearing of gold jewelry and fine clothes. Instead, it should be that of your inner self, the unfading beauty of a gentle and quiet spirit, which is of great worth in God's sight. ~ 1 Peter 4:3-4 NIV

Peter is not saying that braided hair, jewelry or nice clothes are wrong. He's telling us that they stress the outward. God is more interested with what is going on in our heart. Spending time with the LORD produces a gentleness in us that is beautiful.

Daily Inspirations From God's Word

November 22

But the fruit of the Spirit is love, joy, peace, patience, kindness, goodness, faithfulness, gentleness, and self-control.

~ Galatians 5:22-23 NIV

There are nine fruits of the Spirit. Is gentleness one of the fruits others would say is evident in you? If not, ask God to cultivate this one in you.

November 23

My goal is that they may be encouraged in heart and united in love, so that they may have the full riches of understanding, in order that they may know the mystery of God, namely, Christ.

~ Colossians 2:2 NIV

In this letter, Paul spoke to the church at Laodicea, but it applies to all Christians. When false doctrine infiltrates a congregation, it affects the entire church. To encourage one another, we must be united in our love for Christ, not divided. To have the full riches of understanding, we need to study God's Word ourselves and know what it says.

November 24

If you have any encouragement from being united with Christ, if any comfort from his love, if any fellowship with the Spirit, if any tenderness and compassion, then make my joy complete by being like-minded, having the same love, being one in spirit and purpose.

~ Philippians 2:1-2 NIV

If we are united with Christ, then we'll experience encouragement, comfort and fellowship from him. We'll know his tenderness and compassion toward us. This enables us to come together with fellow believers and be like-minded, loving others because we're one in spirit and purpose.

November 25

Also in Judah the hand of God was on the people to give them unity of mind to carry out what the king and his officials had ordered, following the word of the LORD. ~ 2 Chronicles 30:12 NIV

God wanted his people to willingly participate in celebrating the Passover. It was the hand of God that was on the people to give them unity of mind to do what God asked them. Pray for the hand of God to bring unity to your family, your church, your work place, and our nation.

November 26

I in them and you in me. May they be brought to

Daily Inspirations From God's Word

*complete unity to let the world know that you
sent me and have loved them even as you have
loved me.* ~ John 17:23 NIV

Jesus prayed this prayer to the Father for all
believers. We can witness to the world more
effectively if we are unified. How are you
helping to bring unity to your church? Are you
part of the problem, arguing over divisive
matters, or are you striving to work together?
Our witness depends on unity.

November 27

*How good and pleasant it is when brothers live
together in unity!* ~ Psalm 133:1 NIV

We may not always agree with our family,
friends or colleagues, but we can agree to get
along despite our differences of opinion, for
the sake of unity.

Daily Inspirations From God's Word

November 28

May the God who gives endurance and encouragement give you a spirit of unity among yourselves as you follow Christ Jesus, so that with one mouth you may glorify the God and Father of our Lord Jesus Christ.

~ Romans 15:5-6 NIV

Some people – even as Christians – are known for being divisive and argumentative. That should not be. Our goal in following Jesus is to glorify him by staying out of strife. Pray for yourself and others to have a spirit of unity so that Jesus may be glorified.

November 29

Make every effort to keep the unity of the Spirit through the bond of peace.

~ Ephesians 4:3 NIV

Daily Inspirations From God's Word

It is through the Spirit that we have unity and peace. Still, we have a responsibility to do our part. What are you willing to do to keep the unity and peace in your circles? As we focus on God, not ourselves or the circumstances, we grow in unity.

November 30

No one whose hope is in you will ever be put to shame, but they will be put to shame who are treacherous without excuse. ~ Psalm 25:3 NIV

Hoping in God means trusting him. Some put their trust in money, some put their trust in people. But when we put our trust in God, when our hope is in him, we experience his faithfulness.

Daily Inspirations From God's Word

December 1

But the eyes of the LORD are on those who fear him, on those whose hope is in his unfailing love.

~ Psalm 33:18 NIV

What does God see when he looks on us? Is our hope in God or is it in something else? God looks for those who revere him, who are confident of his love for them. Those who hope are certain and sure in their belief of God's unfailing love and faithfulness.

December 2

Why are you downcast, O my soul? Why so disturbed within me? Put your hope in God, for I will yet praise him, my Savior and my God.

~ Psalm 42:5 NIV

In the midst of discouragement, we need to remember that God is there. Keep pressing in,

Daily Inspirations From God's Word

and offer your praise for what he will do. Then wait expectantly with your hope in him.

December 3

Do not let your heart envy sinners, but always be zealous for the fear of the LORD. There is surely a future hope for you, and your hope will not be cut off. ~ Proverbs 23:17-18 NIV

Though you may see people who seem to get away with their sin, don't let that stop you from your pursuit of God. He knows whose hearts are toward him, and he promises a future hope for those who wholeheartedly trust in him.

December 4

Even youths grow tired and weary, and young

Daily Inspirations From God's Word

men stumble and fall; but those who hope in the
LORD will renew their strength. They will soar
on wings like eagles; they will run and not grow
weary, they will walk and not be faint.

~ Isaiah 40:30-31 NIV

Life is demanding, schedules are full, and
people's expectations of us are high. We will
all grow weary at times. But when we expect
God to provide what we need, he will renew
our strength and enable us to soar to heights
we wouldn't have thought possible.

December 5

'For I know the plans I have for you,' declares the
LORD, 'plans to prosper you and not to harm
you, plans to give you hope and a future.'

~ Jeremiah 29:11 NIV

It is encouraging that God knows our future

plans. Some people only see a bleak future. But those who are in God's will, need not be afraid to move ahead with him. God is in control and he has good plans to prosper our future with hope, not harm.

December 6

Yet this I call to mind and therefore I have hope: because of the LORD'S great love we are not consumed, for his compassion's never fail. They are new every morning; great is your faithfulness. ~ Lamentations 3:21-22 NIV

We can have hope in the midst of affliction like Jeremiah did. All may seem lost, and without God it is. But Jeremiah remembered God's great love and he knew all that threatened the people would not consume them. Are you surrounded by circumstances or sin that wants to consume you? Put your hope in God's great love, for he is compassionate and forgiving. His mercies are new every morning. Go to him and see.

December 7

On coming to the house, they saw the child with his mother Mary, and they bowed down and worshiped him. Then they opened their treasures and presented him with gifts of gold and of incense and of myrrh. ~ Matthew 2:11 NIV

The wise men came to see the baby Jesus, the promised Messiah. They bowed down and worshiped him and honored him with costly gifts. People spend a lot of time and money shopping for Christmas gifts for each other. Have you thought about Jesus and what gift you will give to him? He once said, "what you do for one of the least of these, you do for me." (Mathew 25:40.) Ask him to show you what present you can give to him this Christmas.

Daily Inspirations From God's Word

December 8

But to each one of us grace has been given as Christ apportioned it. This is why it says: 'When he ascended on high, he took many captives and gave gifts to his people.' So Christ himself gave the apostles, the prophets, the evangelists, the pastors and the teachers, to equip his people for works of service, so that the body of Christ may be built up. ~ Ephesians 4:7-8,11-12 NIV

Jesus victoriously defeated Satan. Jesus was willing to descend to the depths to defeat him, and when he ascended on high Jesus, like every triumphant conqueror, took captives. He conquered and took captive sin, the devil and death. He then gave gifts to his people for their edification. What a mighty God we serve. Have you thanked him for the gifts he's given?

Daily Inspirations From God's Word

December 9

This salvation, which was first announced by the Lord, was confirmed to us by those who heard him. God also testified to it by signs, wonders and various miracles, and gifts of the Holy Spirit distributed according to his will.

~ Hebrews 2:3b-4 NIV

Many times, Jesus announced to the disciples that salvation would come through him. The disciples were eyewitnesses to it. Future generations all the way down to us, believe by faith on the disciples' account. We also believe by God's testimony through signs, wonders, miracles and gifts of the Holy Spirit. All of these authenticate the Gospel.

December 10

But only the high priest entered the inner room, and that only once a year, and never without

Daily Inspirations From God's Word

blood, which he offered for himself and for the sins the people had committed in ignorance. The Holy Spirit was showing by this that the way into the Most Holy Place had not yet been disclosed as long as the first tabernacle was still standing. This is an illustration for the present time, indicating that the gifts and sacrifices being offered were not able to clear the conscience of the worshiper. ~ Hebrews 9:7-9NIV

In the Old Testament, the high priest was a symbol of what was to come. He was the only one who could enter the inner room of the Tabernacle and the only one allowed access to God. He brought blood on the people's behalf for their sins. In the New Testament, and under the new covenant, Jesus came to fulfill the law. All people gained access to God through the gift and sacrifice of Jesus' shed blood, therefore no longer needing an earthly priest.

Daily Inspirations From God's Word

December 11

Make vows to the LORD your God and fulfill them; let all the neighboring lands bring gifts to the One to be feared. ~ Psalm 76:11 NIV

In prayer, we often ask God to fulfill all our wants and needs. This verse challenges us to make vows or promises to the LORD and then carry them out. Have you ever promised God that you would serve him in some way, then didn't follow through once you began? He is worthy of our very best. What gifts can you bring to him of your, time, talent and treasure? Will you let God use them to help others?

December 12

Good will come to him who is generous and lends freely. He has scattered abroad his gifts to the poor; his righteousness endures forever;

Daily Inspirations From God's Word

their horn will be lifted high in honor.

~ Psalm 112:5,9 NIV

If we let worries about our money stop us from giving, we rob ourselves of the blessing that comes from giving. But when we trust God, who supplies all of our needs, we will give generously to others. God honors those who share their gifts with those less fortunate. Will you be one He honors?

December 13

There are different kinds of gifts, but the same Spirit distributes them. There are different kinds of service, but the same Lord. There are different kinds of working, but in all of them and in everyone it is the same God at work.

~ 1 Corinthians 12:4 NIV

Daily Inspirations From God's Word

Paul stresses that although there are differences in our gifts, the same Spirit – the same God – distributes to all for the benefit of the body. Don't let differences hinder your fellowship in the body of Christ. We are all one in Him.

December 14

For God so loved the world that he gave his one and only Son, that whoever believes in him shall not perish but have eternal life. ~ John 3:16 NIV

The birth of a baby born in a manger was the Father's love gift to the world. The culmination of that gift resulted in our Lord freely giving his life for ours. There is no greater love than the sacrificial death of Jesus Christ so that we who believe can live in eternity.

Daily Inspirations From God's Word

December 15

"Because he loves me," says the LORD, "I will rescue him; I will protect him, for he acknowledges my name." ~ Psalm 91:14 NIV

We show our love for God by following him and spending time with him. When we acknowledge him, he notices. We live in a dangerous world and no one receives the guarantee of a life free of trouble. But when we call upon God, we can trust him to help us in our time of need.

December 16

The LORD your God is with you, the Mighty Warrior who saves. He will take great delight in you, he will quiet you with his love, he will rejoice over you with his singing.

~ Zephaniah 3:17 NIV

God reminded the people through Zephaniah that He was with them. His love restores. As a mother who sings over her children, quiets them with her love, and takes great delight in them, so God rejoices over you with His singing because you are His.

December 17

But God demonstrates his own love for us in this: While we were still sinners, Christ died for us.

~ Romans 5:8 NIV

How amazing it is to ponder that Christ died for sinners. When children do wrong, they grieve their parents' heart, but the parent still loves them. How much more does God show his love for us, his sinning children, by sending his Son to die in our place.

Daily Inspirations From God's Word

December 18

You have heard that it was said, 'Love your neighbor and hate your enemy.' But I tell you: Love your enemies and pray for those who persecute you. ~ Matthew 5:43-44 NIV

Sometimes we make an enemy of our spouse, sibling, parent, or an estranged friend. Those who've hurt us may be hurting too. What can you do when nothing in you wants to love your enemy. Ask God to help you love them, the way he loves you. Ask God to help you forgive the offense and then pray for them. Then watch what God – in time – unfolds.

December 19

This is how we know what love is: Jesus Christ laid down his life for us. And we ought to lay down our lives for our brothers.

~ 1 John 3:16 NIV

Daily Inspirations From God's Word

Jesus is our example in how to love sacrificially. Most parents show love to their families by giving of themselves, serving, and putting others first. We show sacrificial love by listening, encouraging, and helping others at a cost to us – usually our time. What are you willing to sacrifice for love?

December 20

How great is the love the Father has lavished on us, that we should be called children of God!

~ 1 John 3:1 NIV

An orphan knows the great joy of being called somebody's child. The adoptive parent doesn't love them only a little; they show that child great amounts of love. Do you realize how much God loves you and how much you – His adopted child – mean to him? Oh, that we would know the depths of his love for us.

Daily Inspirations From God's Word

December 21

For he chose us in him before the creation of the world to be holy and blameless in his sight. In love he predestined us for adoption to sonship, through Jesus Christ. ~ Ephesians 1:4-5 NIV

Adopted children don't choose their parents. They are the chosen ones. God had a plan for our salvation before we even existed. He chose to adopt us into his family by our faith in his Son, Jesus Christ. It is not by any work we do, but by what we believe that we receive this sonship.

December 22

Simon Peter answered, "You are the Christ, the son of the living God." ~ Matthew 16:16 NIV

The disciples spent day and night for three years with Jesus. They saw his great power and wisdom. Jesus asked his disciples who they believed him to be. Peter was first to understand and proclaim him to be the Christ. As you spend time with God, studying his Word, you begin to understand who Jesus really is. Have you, like Peter, proclaimed Jesus Christ to be the Son of the living God?

December 23

Jesus did many other miraculous signs in the presence of his disciples, which are not recorded in this book. But these are written that you may believe that Jesus is the Christ, the Son of God, and that by believing you may have life in his name. ~ John 20:30-31 NIV

The written accounts of all that Jesus did, recorded by eyewitnesses, are called the Gospels. These were left so that we who came after his death would also believe in him. Eternal life comes only through faith that

Daily Inspirations From God's Word

Jesus Christ is God's Son, sent by Him to redeem the world.

December 24

This is how the birth of Jesus Christ came about: His mother Mary was pledged to be married to Joseph, but before they came together, she was found to be with child through the Holy Spirit.

~ Matthew 1:18 NIV

The miraculous birth of Jesus was also scandalous. No one before or since has ever become pregnant by the Holy Spirit. The birth of God's Son was unique. The faith of the young virgin and her fiancée' was tested. God gave them a high calling and a great privilege to raise His Son. How is your faith stirred by these miraculous events?

Daily Inspirations From God's Word

December 25

Today in the town of David a Savior has been born to you; he is Christ the Lord.

~ Luke 2:11 NIV

For four hundred years, the people of Israel awaited the birth of the promised Messiah. He came quietly in the night. An angel announced his birth to the nearby shepherds in the field. God keeps his promises. Tell everyone that this day we celebrate the birth of our Savior, the Lord Jesus Christ.

December 26

Now there was a man in Jerusalem called Simeon, who was righteous and devout. It had been revealed to him by the Holy Spirit that he would not die before he had seen the Lord's Christ. Simeon took him in his arms and praised God, saying: Sovereign Lord, as you have promised, you may now dismiss your servant in peace. For my eyes have seen your salvation.

~ Luke 2:25-26, 28-30 NIV

Jewish parents brought their babies to the temple and presented them to the Lord. When Joseph and Mary brought baby Jesus, they met the old man Simeon. God revealed to Simeon through the Holy Spirit that this baby was the Messiah. What is God revealing to you?

December 27

But in your hearts revere Christ as Lord. Always be prepared to give an answer to everyone who asks you to give the reason for the hope that you have. But do this with gentleness and respect.

~ 1 Peter 3:15 NIV

When your life shows devotion for the Lord Jesus Christ, people will notice a difference, and ask you about it. How are you prepared to explain what Christ has done in your life? Can you explain in a way that isn't preachy, but shows the hope you have in Christ?

December 28

I know that you can do all things; no plan of yours can be thwarted. ~ Job 42:2 NIV

God is Sovereign. We may not understand why he allows certain things to happen. Circumstances can lead us to question God's Sovereignty, but faith trusts that God is in control. It does not matter how the present looks-his plans will prevail.

December 29

Many are the plans in a person's heart, but it is the Lord's purpose that prevails.

~ Proverbs 19:21

Daily Inspirations From God's Word

Some people make plans and then ask God to bless them. No matter how many plans a person makes, God will have his way. Pray and listen for God's leading in your life.

December 30
Hear my voice when I call, O LORD, be merciful to me and answer me. ~ Psalm 27:7NIV

It is good to seek God's guidance for the coming year. Call out to him, and pray for God-directed paths.

December 31
Show me your ways, O LORD, teach me your paths; guide me in your truth and teach me.

~ Psalm 25:4-5 NIV

Daily Inspirations From God's Word

Is it your desire to know God more next year than you did this year? Then ask him to show you and teach you how to follow him. Determine to read and study your Bible on a daily basis. As you do, God will guide you and grow your faith.

ABOUT THE AUTHOR

Doreen Wennberg has been involved
in women's ministry since 1999.
As an avid Bible student, she is
equally passionate about teaching
the truths in God's Word.

Other titles by Doreen Wennberg:
Newlywed Book of Prayers
Praying For Your New Spouse
The Husband's Version

Newlywed Book of Prayers
Praying For Your New Spouse
The Wife's Version
Both available on Amazon
or
doreenwennberg.com

Daily Inspirations From God's Word

Daily Inspirations From God's Word

CPSIA information can be obtained
at www.ICGtesting.com
Printed in the USA
BVHW040022091118
532574BV00014B/82/P